Financial Fitness for Life

Shaping Up Your Financial Future

Grades 6–8

Student Workouts

Barbara Flowers
Sheryl Szot Gallaher

NCEE

National Council on Economic Education

Authors:

Barbara Flowers is the Assistant Director of the Center for Entrepreneurship and Economic Education at the University of Missouri-St. Louis. She has worked on numerous economic education publications.

Sheryl Szot Gallaher is the Director of the Office of Economic Education at Governors State University in University Park, Illinois. She was formerly a classroom teacher, Gifted Education Coordinator, and economic education consultant for the Illinois Council on Economic Education.

Project Director:

John E. Clow is the Director of the Leatherstocking Center for Economic Education at the State University of New York, College at Oneonta and Professor Emeritus of that college. He is a national award-winning college teacher, speaker, and author in the fields of personal finance, economics, and business education.

Design:

Roher/Sprague Partners

This publication was made possible through funding by the Bank of America Foundation.

ISBN 1-56183-545-5

TABLE OF CONTENTS

THEME 3:

Tomorrow's Money: Getting to the End of the Rainbow
(Saving)

THEME 1

There Is No Such Thing as a Free Lunch

(The Economic Way of Thinking)

Introduction

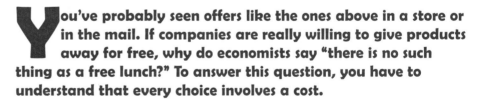

You've probably seen offers like the ones above in a store or in the mail. If companies are really willing to give products away for free, why do economists say "there is no such thing as a free lunch?" To answer this question, you have to understand that every choice involves a cost.

Because time, space, and money are limited, and human wants are unlimited, people cannot have everything they want. When people cannot have everything they want, they have to make choices, and when they make a choice, they must give something up. The next best alternative that is given up when a choice is made is the opportunity cost.

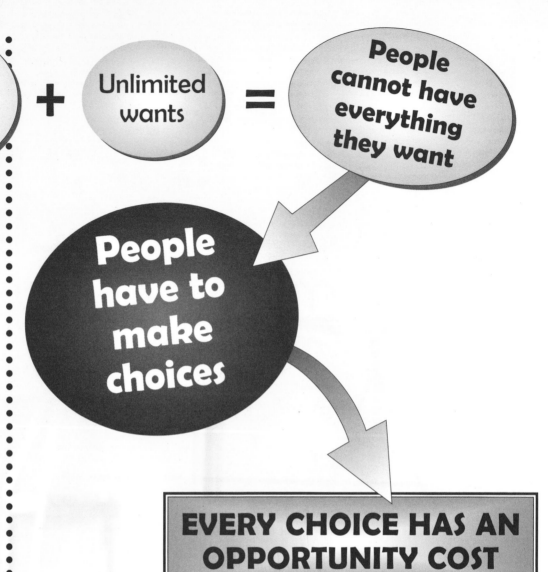

Limited time, space, and money

+

Unlimited wants

=

People cannot have everything they want

People have to make choices

EVERY CHOICE HAS AN OPPORTUNITY COST

That's why there's no free lunch—or free CDs.
There is always an opportunity cost.

When you make decisions, you need to consider, in a logical way, the opportunity cost of your choices. By using the *economic way of thinking* and by developing a good decision-making plan, you'll be able to evaluate your options and make better choices.

2

LESSON 1
The Economic Way of Thinking

Warm-Up

Often, when you talk to a friend or relative, you learn about situations that make you scratch your head and ask, "Why would a person do this?" Here are some examples:

▲ A college student runs up $30,000 in credit card debt.

▲ A store marks down summer jackets from $300 to only $39.95 in October.

▲ Voters defeat a plan to finance a football stadium with property tax revenues.

Unlocking the secrets of these situations might be easier if you applied the economic way of thinking to determine WHY people act the way they do.

In this lesson, you will learn how to use the economic way of thinking, a process that can help you understand why people save, borrow, and spend the way they do. It will also help you make wise money decisions by examining the way you yourself think and act.

FITNESS VOCABULARY

Opportunity Cost – The next-best alternative that is given up when a choice is made.

Incentive – A reason or reward that motivates people to behave in predictable ways.

Consequence – The result or effect of a person's behavior.

3

MUSCLE DEVELOPERS

Learn these ideas, practice them, and develop your financial fitness muscles.

✔ The **economic way of thinking** provides a method for analyzing people's behavior.

✔ Because time, space, and money are limited, and wants are unlimited, people can't have everything they want.

✔ People must make *choices*.

✔ Every choice involves a *cost*.

✔ People respond to *incentives*.

✔ Choices have *consequences*.

Showing Your Strength

If you know the answers to these questions, you are developing some financial muscle.

1 **Why should people use the economic way of thinking?** *(By examining the costs and benefits of decisions, people will be more likely to make good decisions.)*

2 **Why do people have to make choices?** *(Resources are limited, and wants are unlimited; people cannot have everything they want. That's why they have to choose.)*

3 **Why do economists say "there's no such thing as a free lunch"?** *(Nothing is free, because every choice involves an opportunity cost.)*

4 **How do incentives work?** *(Incentives are rewards [both monetary and non-monetary] that motivate behavior. Because people tend to respond to incentives in predictable ways, sometimes people's behavior can be changed by offering incentives. For example, if Mom says "I'll pay you $5.00 if you'll baby-sit for your brother," the $5.00 is a monetary incentive. If Mom says "You can stay out an hour later tomorrow if you'll baby-sit for your brother today," the extra hour is a non-monetary incentive.)*

5 **What is a disincentive?** *(Just the opposite of an incentive; it is not a reward but a penalty. Many drivers slow down when they see a police car because getting a $100 fine is a pretty powerful disincentive.)*

6 **What are consequences?** *(The results of behaviors are consequences. Studying for a test usually results in a good grade; the good grade is a consequence.)*

Every Choice Has An Opportunity Cost

Because of limited resources and unlimited wants, people have to make choices. Every choice has an opportunity cost.

In each situation below, a person must make choices because of limited time, space, and/or money. Below each description, list the person's alternatives, the choice, and the opportunity cost.

Shaundra's mother's birthday is coming up. Shaundra would like to buy her mom a necklace, but the one she likes costs more than she has saved. What are Shaundra's alternatives? What will she do? What's her opportunity cost?

Alternatives: _____

_____

Choice: _____

Opportunity Cost: _____

_____

5

Angelo wants to put a 50-gallon aquarium in his room. When he measured the room, Angelo discovered that he wouldn't have enough space for his stereo and the aquarium. What are Angelo's alternatives? What will he do? What's his opportunity cost?

Alternatives: _____

_____

Choice: _____

Opportunity Cost: _____

_____

_____

Raul has raised $200 for a local charity. If he raises $15 more, he will be eligible for a raffle for a new computer. The raffle is tomorrow. What are Raul's alternatives? What will he do? What's his opportunity cost?

Alternatives: _____

_____

Choice: _____

Opportunity Cost: _____

_____

_____

_____

_____

Grand Prize!

Choosing the Better Incentive

This activity focuses on price, a powerful monetary (or economic) incentive. Working with a partner, evaluate the pairs of coupons/ incentives for the 10 purchases below and, for each one, choose the one that provides greater benefit. Then, on the reply sheet, explain how you arrived at your decision.

#1 COUPON 20% off

1. Bookbag: $11.99 (buy one)

The better incentive is coupon #

The reason is:

#2 COUPON Save $2.00

#1 COUPON Buy 2 Get 1 FREE!

2. Snappy-Krunch Cereal:
$2.59 per box (buy three boxes)

The better incentive is coupon #

The reason is:

#2 COUPON Save $1.00 per box

7

3. Super-Nutty Peanut Butter:

32 oz. jar for $2.56 or 48 oz. jar
for $2.99 (buy two jars, either size)

The better incentive is coupon #

The reason is:

#1 COUPON

Buy a 32-oz. jar
at regular price,
get another **free!**

#2 COUPON

Save $0.50 on each 48-oz. jar

#1 COUPON

Buy one pair –
Get another at
HALF PRICE!

#2 COUPON

2 pairs for $100.00

4. Soccer shoes: $69.95 a pair
(buy two pairs)

The better incentive is coupon #

The reason is:

5. Amusement park: All day
admission ticket, $45.00 (buy 6 tickets)

The better incentive is coupon #

The reason is:

#1 COUPON

$5 off each ticket (limit 6)
when you buy a case of
root beer at $7.99 a case

#2 COUPON

Buy 5 tickets at regular
price, get the 6th one
FREE

#1 COUPON
Save 10% on 3 hours

#2 COUPON
Save $0.50 each hour up to 2 hours; Save $0.25 each hour after that

6. Internet coffee shop:

$6 per hour (pay for 3 hours)

The better incentive is coupon # _____

The reason is: _____

7. Scary movie festival: $8.00 each night for 6 nights (attend all 6 nights)

The better incentive is coupon # _____

The reason is: _____

#1 COUPON
4 nights at regular price; half price the next two nights

#2 COUPON
5 nights at regular price – 6th night FREE

#1 COUPON
Save $2.00 on each pizza
Limit 2

8. Pizza: $18.99 (buy 2 pizzas)

The better incentive is coupon # _____

The reason is: _____

#2 COUPON
Today only: 2 pizzas $35

#1

COUPON
REBATE
$14.00 each
Limit 2

#2

COUPON
Save 20%
NO LIMIT

9. Video game: $49.99 (buy 3 games)

The better incentive is coupon #

The reason is:

10. Candy bars: 2 oz. for $0.89;
4 oz. for $1.69 (buy 12 oz of candy)

The better incentive is coupon #

The reason is:

#1

COUPON
Buy 2 4-oz. Bars at
regular price
Get a 2-oz. bar FREE

#2

COUPON
Save $0.20
on every
2-oz. bar

Financial Fitness for Life: Shaping Up Your Financial Future Student Workouts, ©National Council on Economic Education

EXERCISE 1.3

Using the Economic Way of Thinking

Read the following situation. Then use the **economic way of thinking** to analyze the people's behaviors.

Susan B. Anthony Middle School's Honor Society was planning a dance. A music committee was formed to decide whether to use a local DJ or a video/sound show. The committee decided on the video-sound show, even though the price was $300 higher than the local DJ. By paying for the video/sound show, the students believed they could attract more students to the dance.

Finally, when the big night arrived, 250 students from a class of 300 attended the dance, which was the greatest number any dance had ever attracted. The Honor Society was pleased with the results of its fundraiser.

1 The committee could not choose both the DJ and the video show? Why not? What was limited? _____

2 What did the committee choose?

_____

3 What was the incentive for its choice?

_____

4 What was the opportunity cost?

_____

5 What were the costs and benefits of the choice?

_____

6 List one or two consequences of the choice.

_____

7 What did the committee think would happen as a result of its decision?

_____

On the next page, write another decision-making story, along with questions like the ones above. Challenge your classmates to analyze your story, using the **economic way of thinking.**

ASSESSMENT

1.1

The Economic Way of Thinking

A. Examine the decisions made by the people in the following situations by using the economic way of thinking.

1 Instead of putting an extra $3,000 in their retirement fund, Florence and Joe decided to fly from Chicago to Florida for a week of golf and relaxation.

▲ Choice:_____

▲ Opportunity cost:_____

▲ Incentive: _____

▲ Suggest a consequence of their choice: _____

_____

▲ How did Florence and Joe benefit from their choice?_____

_____

2 Brian and Sheryl paid their credit card debt instead of putting a down payment on a new convertible.

▲ Choice:_____

▲ Opportunity cost:_____

▲ Incentive: _____

▲ Suggest a consequence of their choice: _____

_____

▲ How did Brian and Sheryl benefit from their choice?_____

_____

3 Su-Zee, Lorena, and their friends went to the beach instead of working at the school book sale last weekend.

▲ Choice:_____

▲ Opportunity cost:_____

▲ Incentive: _____

▲ Suggest a consequence of their choice: _____

_____

▲ How did Su-Zee, Lorena, and their friends benefit from their choice?_____

_____

13

B. Use the economic way of thinking to identify "Why math teachers give homework every day." Consider that the teacher will have to correct the homework, and will have less time for other activities. Think of incentives and consequences for both teacher and students that result from the teacher giving homework every day.

▲ Teacher's Choice: _____

▲ Opportunity cost: _____

▲ Incentive for making the choice: _____

_____

▲ Suggest a consequence of the choice: _____

_____

▲ How/who benefits? _____

_____

LESSON 2
Consumer Decision Making

Warm-Up

Back in your grandparents' days, corner grocery stores carried one or two brands of breakfast cereal, laundry detergent, and soft drinks. It was pretty easy then to decide what to buy with your hard-earned money.

Today's supermarkets and mega-malls are different; they offer thousands of choices. That's good because it provides variety in your life, but it also makes choosing more difficult.

When you go shopping, how do you decide what to buy? Do you pick the first box of cookies you see on a shelf? Do you simply choose the brand you've always bought, without checking out any new products? Or are you a careful shopper who compares ingredients and prices?

This lesson introduces you to a plan that will help you make decisions. The PACED decision-making process is a step-by-step strategy that you can use for making all kinds of choices—the right pair of jeans or basketball shoes, or the best way to spend your time on a Saturday night. Being able to make well-thought-out decisions will start you on the right path toward a lifetime of good choices.

FITNESS VOCABULARY

Opportunity Cost – The next-best alternative that is given up when a choice is made.

Trade-Off – Giving up a little of one thing in order to get a little more of something else.

Alternatives – Options to be considered when making a decision.

Criteria – Measures or requirements by which alternatives are judged.

Cost/benefit analysis – comparing advantages and disadvantages in order to make a decision.

Financial Fitness for Life: Shaping Up Your Financial Future Student Workouts, ©National Council on Economic Education

The PACED Decision-Making Process includes the following steps:

▲ State the **P**roblem.

▲ List **A**lternatives.

▲ Identify **C**riteria.

▲ **E**valuate Alternatives.

▲ Make a **D**ecision.

Analyzing costs and benefits, as part of the PACED decision-making process, enables a person to make rational decisions. A rational decision is thought out and based on facts; the opposite would be an impulsive, spur-of-the-moment, emotional decision.

MUSCLE DEVELOPERS
Learn these ideas, practice them, and develop your financial fitness muscles.

✔ Every choice involves an opportunity cost.

✔ Decisions often involve trade-offs: giving up a little of something in order to get more of something else. (For example, you might have two hours free on a Saturday afternoon. You could spend two hours playing basketball and give up studying for a big test, or you might choose to give up an hour of basketball in order to spend an hour studying.)

Showing Your Strength

If you know the answers to these questions, you are developing some financial muscle.

1 **Why do people have to make choices?** *(Because resources are limited, you can't have everything you want. So you have to choose.)*

2 **How can you be sure your choice is a good one?** *(Making rational choices is easy if you have a plan. The PACED decision-making process can help you make wise choices.)*

3 **Why is it important to use a decision-making process such as PACED?** *(When you use a plan to make decisions, you begin to think rationally about WHY you are doing what you are doing. As you use the plan for small decisions, you'll become better and better at it. Then, when a big, important choice comes up, you'll be prepared, and make a good decision.)*

4 **After you make a decision, is that the end?** *(Not really. Sometimes you will want to examine the outcome of your decision and re-evaluate your choice.)*

5 **What is cost/benefit analysis?** *(It means looking at the advantages and disadvantages of your alternatives. For example, if your alternatives for Monday night are baby-sitting for $20 or going to the mall with your friends, there are costs and benefits associated with each. If you go to the mall, what's the cost? [You miss out on the $20 baby-sitting money]. What's the benefit? (You get to enjoy being with your friends.] If you baby-sit, what's the cost? [Not being with friends.] What's the benefit? [Having spending money.] When the benefit outweighs the cost, it's a good decision.)*

EXERCISE 2.1

Which Graham Cracker Is Best?

▲ Use A, B, and C in the first column to identify your alternatives (different crackers).

▲ List the characteristics by which you will judge the item across the top row (criteria).

▲ Evaluate the alternatives using your criteria.
Use the following scoring:
  1 = lowest (or worst)
  2 = middle
  3 = highest (or best)

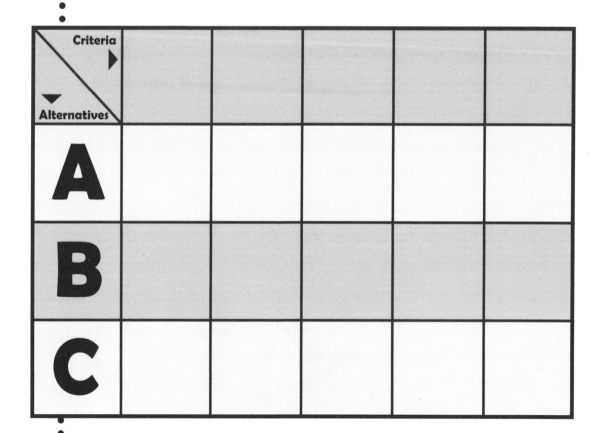

EXERCISE 2.2

Using the PACED Decision-Making Process

Use the PACED decision-making process to make a decision for Marcus and Jeff in the story below:

Marcus and Jeff had $80 each and wanted to buy new baseball mitts. They saw two ads in the newspaper for stores in a nearby shopping mall:

Super-Star Sporting Goods Store

SALE

Selected Baseball Mitts
$65.99

All Sales Final.
No Refunds or Exchanges
Sale ends Saturday

Pro-Athlete Sporting Goods Store

SALE

All Baseball Mitts
$75.99

Satisfaction Guaranteed or your money back (Must have receipt for refunds.)

Complete the questions and the grid as you work through the PACED process.

P What is the problem? (List in space above grid.)

A What are the alternatives? (List them in the first column.)

C Name six criteria that Marcus and Jeff might consider when making their decision. (Put one in each cell in the row marked criteria.)

E Evaluate the alternatives, using the criteria you named, using "yes" or "no" in each cell.

D Make a decision. What should they do? (List in space below grid.)

Problem: _____

_____

_____

Criteria ▶ Alternatives ▼						

What is their decision? _____

_____

_____

_____

What is the opportunity cost? _____

_____

_____

_____

_____

_____

Financial Fitness for Life: Shaping Up Your Financial Future Student Workouts, ©National Council on Economic Education

EXERCISE
2.3

Some Criteria Are More Valuable Than Others

The Noga Family decided it was time to get rid of their old computer and buy a new one. They made a list of criteria that were important in their decision-making plan. After the list was compiled, they agreed that some characteristics of the computer were more important than others, so they gave more value to some criteria than to others. For example, a 17-inch monitor was more important to them than a color printer, and a 56K modem was more important than a stereo sound system. Here's how the values looked in their **PACED** grid:

Read the ads on the next page. Then, using the PACED grid, help the Noga family decide which computer will be the best choice for them, based upon the values of their criteria.

CRITERIA	VALUE
Less than $2000	5 points
17-inch monitor or larger	5 points
Color Printer	4 points
Stereo Sound System	1 point
56K Modem or faster	4 points
128 MB RAM or more	3 points
10 GB Hard Drive or more	2 points

Financial Fitness for Life: Shaping Up Your Financial Future Student Workouts, ©National Council on Economic Education

EXERCISE 2.3 CONTINUED

A

It's the Computer of Your Dreams!

128 MB RAM
Color Printer
17" Monitor
10 GB Hard Drive
Stereo Sound
28 K Modem

$2100

B

Here's the Computer for YOU

✓ $1899.00
✓ 8 GB Hard Drive
✓ 64 MB RAM
✓ Color Printer
✓ 17" Monitor
✓ Stereo Sound
✓ 28 K Modem

C

Tired of waiting while your old computer boots up? Time to move up to a new model!

56 K modem • Color Printer
128 MB RAM • 15" Monitor
8 GB Hard Drive

Only $1999

E

Looking for a Computer? Here it is!!

B & W Laser Printer / 15" Monitor
12 GB Hard Drive / 128 MB RAM
Stereo Sound / 28 K Modem
$1899.00

D

Look no further! We're your Number One Computer Store

❑ 10 GB Hard Drive
❑ 64 MB RAM
❑ $1699.00
❑ 17" Monitor
❑ Stereo Sound
❑ Color Printer
❑ 56K Modem

F

YOU'LL WONDER HOW YOU EVER LIVED WITHOUT THIS NEW COMPUTER SYSTEM!

❖ Color Printer
❖ Stereo Sound
❖ 10 GB Hard Drive
❖ 128 MB RAM
❖ $1399.00
❖ 56k Modem

17" monitor sold separately

G

A New Computer! No Money Down! No Interest! 12 months to pay!

10 GB Hard Drive
128 MB RAM
17" Monitor
Color Printer
Stereo Sound
56 K Modem

Only $175/month

H

So Easy to Install – You'll be Surfing the Net in 10 minutes

Color Printer
17" Monitor
64 MB RAM
10 GB Hard Drive
56K Modem
$1799.00

Using Different Values in the PACED Decision-Making Grid

Criteria ▶	Less than $2000	17" monitor or larger	Stereo sound system	56K modem or faster	128 meg RAM	10 GB hard drive	Color printer	Total Value
Value — Alternatives	5	5	1	4	3	2	4	
A								
B								
C								
D								
E								
F								
G								
H								

1. Which computer should the Noga family buy, based on your grid?

_____

2. Write a sentence or two explaining why the Noga family should buy the computer you suggested.

_____

_____

_____

_____

ASSESSMENT

Panel Discussion

Have you ever wondered how several groups, with similar information, can make different decisions about the same issue? It's probably because each group's criteria are different.

In this exercise, your group will evaluate an issue based upon criteria that are important to you. Then you will plan a panel discussion of the issue, based upon your group's concerns. (You can enhance your group's point of view by doing research, too.) In a political debate, such as this one, the side that gets the most votes wins; however, in this exercise it is not as important to win as it is to state clear and powerful arguments for your choice.

Your teacher will assign you to Group A, Group B, or Group C. Imagine that you are a person in that age group with the concerns listed on the group card. As a group, review your concerns and decide which position your group will support [i.e., (1) library and lab, (2) pool and rec center, (3) senior citizen housing facility]. Each person in your group should write a clear statement supporting one of the group's concerns (conducting extra research will help support your argument).

Issue:

Should your town construct:

1 a library and computer lab, or

2 a swimming pool and recreation center, or

3 a senior citizen housing facility

on 10 acres of vacant land?

Group A

AGE   13–29
CONCERNS   Year-round activity
Athletic opportunities
Health and fitness
Social gatherings
Organized competitive games

Group B

AGE   30–54
CONCERNS   Education
Employment opportunities
Access to information
Investment reports
Details about travel opportunities

Group C

AGE   55–70
CONCERNS   Retirement benefits
Low cost housing opportunities
Health care
Contact with others of same age
Companionship (especially
widowed person)

After the groups have considered their criteria and applied them to the alternatives, each group will present a panel discussion to the class. Be sure to include information about the **alternatives** available, the **criteria** that are important to your group, your method of **evaluating the alternatives**, and your final **decision** for how the vacant land should be used. You may include posters, illustrations, charts, graphs, or a multi-media slide show to enhance your group's presentation.

When all groups are finished, discuss the effectiveness of each group's arguments and of their presentations.

THEME

2

Education Pays Off: Learn Something

(Earning Income)

Introduction

There's an old saying that "great oaks from tiny acorns grow." The meaning is simple: great achievements begin small. Then they blossom and flourish.

Education and financial security are good examples of how this works in life. Doing well in the elementary grades, studying all through middle school, graduating from high school, and continuing your education are the little steps that usually result in a big payoff: an enjoyable job with a good income.

The best way to increase your chances for a good income in a career you enjoy is to begin planning NOW. Think about what you like to do in your spare time. Do you like to write stories, fix broken toys, play the trumpet, or gaze through a telescope? Don't worry if the things you enjoy are different from the activities your classmates find appealing. Everybody is unique. But by examining your options, and finding out about careers that will be in demand in the future, you'll be able to make choices that can lead to a good income in an occupation you truly enjoy.

LESSON 3
Career Decision Making

Warm-Up

Scott Turow earned his law degree and was a successful attorney; then he decided to write novels. One of his books, Presumed Innocent, **was made into a successful TV movie. Bill Bradley was a professional basketball player. When his playing days were over, he ran successfully for election to the U.S. Senate and even took a shot at the White House in 2000. Oprah Winfrey began her career as a news reporter. Now she owns her own production company, acts in movies, and teaches at a university.**

How could these people be so successful in such different careers? The answer is simple. They all learned from their experiences and applied their expertise to new situations. Scott Turow's legal know-how influenced his novels about courts and justice. The teamwork and discipline Bill Bradley learned playing basketball enabled him to develop and carry out a successful political campaign in his state. And Oprah Winfrey's ability to relate to all kinds of people as a broadcaster enhanced her success in other arenas too.

FITNESS VOCABULARY

SCANS skills – Guidelines for workplace success (developed by the Department of Labor **S**ecretary's **C**ommission on **A**chieving **N**ecessary **S**kills.)

Self-assessment – Examining characteristics about yourself.

Career cluster – Jobs within a similar category, e.g., artist and graphic designer, bookkeeper and accountant, chef and dietitian.

Work ethic – Determination and positive habits on the job. Positive habits include reliability, punctuality, friendliness, honesty, and ability to work independently or in cooperation with others.

Entrepreneur – A person who takes a risk to create a business in order to earn a profit.

Human capital – Knowledge, skills, experience, and attitude that help a person do a job better.

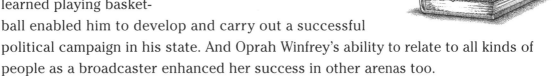

27

In any job, you have to solve problems, deal with different personalities and make customers feel special. Once learned, these lessons can be practiced in other occupations. Business millionaires such as Steve Case (*America Online*), Jeff Bezos (*Amazon.com*) and Jim Kelly (*United Parcel Service*) started out in ordinary jobs. Case scooped ice cream, Bezos flipped burgers, and Kelly drove a delivery truck. But their experiences taught them responsibility, dependability, and reliability. Later they were able to apply these and other acquired skills to new jobs, and eventually they became leaders in their companies.

You don't have to be rich and famous to recognize that the skills and experience you gain in one career can be utilized in another. In this lesson, you will learn how to examine and evaluate your own qualities so that you will be able to choose a path that will provide a variety of options for both job satisfaction and a good income.

MUSCLE DEVELOPERS
Learn these ideas, practice them, and develop your financial fitness muscles.

✔ Applying basic skills, working on a team, communicating effectively, solving problems, and using resources and technology—all are necessary for success in today's workplace.

✔ Knowing about yourself—your likes and dislikes—and evaluating alternatives can help you choose the right career.

✔ Investing in your human capital increases the likelihood of being successful in your chosen occupation.

✔ Demonstrating a good and positive work ethic will make you an asset to an employer.

✔ Some people will be successful and satisfied working for someone else. Others —entrepreneurs—find their greatest satisfaction in being their own boss.

✔ Entrepreneurs help keep the engine of a market economy running.

Showing Your Strength

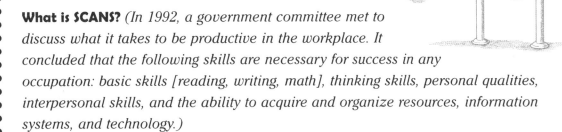

If you know the answers to these questions, you are developing some financial muscle.

1 **What is SCANS?** *(In 1992, a government committee met to discuss what it takes to be productive in the workplace. It concluded that the following skills are necessary for success in any occupation: basic skills [reading, writing, math], thinking skills, personal qualities, interpersonal skills, and the ability to acquire and organize resources, information systems, and technology.)*

2 **What are some major categories to examine when assessing your own likes and dislikes in the workplace?** *(Ask yourself if you enjoy working with people, data, things or ideas. Knowing this can help lead you in the direction of a satisfying career.)*

3 **What are career clusters?** *(Categories of occupations that have characteristics in common.)*

4 **Why should you consider career clusters?** *(By focusing on a cluster of careers instead of a single one, more options remain available. That way, if you think you want to be a doctor, but later find out it's not for you, you might use the training you've already completed to become an X-ray technician, a lab assistant, or even a writer in a medical journal.)*

5 **Why should a person develop a good work ethic?** *(Many employers look first for employees with good attitudes and good work habits. They find that it is easier to teach employees the skills needed for a specific job than it is to train people to be pleasant, friendly, punctual, and responsible.)*

6 **Why are entrepreneurs important in an economy?** *(Entrepreneurs are the innovators who notice a problem, help to solve or alleviate the problem by producing a good or service, and turn it into a business opportunity. They are independent, hard-working risk-takers who develop products and help create jobs.)*

7 **How can a person invest in her or his own human capital?** *(By taking the right classes in school, learning on the job, and accepting a summer position as a non-paid intern. A person can acquire the knowledge, skills, experience, and attitude to do a job better through these experiences. Enhanced human capital can lead to more career opportunities.)*

Financial Fitness for Life: Shaping Up Your Financial Future Student Workouts, ©National Council on Economic Education

Demand for Labor in Various Occupational Areas

The chart on this page shows the Bureau of Labor Statistics' employment figures for 1998 and projected employment figures for the year 2008. Work with your teammates to calculate the number and percentage increase (+) or decrease (–) for each occupational area listed.

A	B	C	D	E
INDUSTRY	**Actual number employed in 1998**	**Projected number employed in 2008**	**Change in number from 1998–2008 (Col C – Column B)** Indicate + or –	**Percentage change 1998–2008 (Col D / Column B)** Indicate + or –
Education	11,174,900	12,884,700		
Hospitals	4,909,200	5,284,900		
Savings institutions	1,904,900	1,932,000		
Federal gov't	1,819,100	1,654,600		
Nursing facilities	1,762,000	2,212,900		
Computer services	1,599,300	3,471,300		
Agriculture, forestry, fishing	1,154,000	1,006,200		
Legal services	972,500	1,200,000		
Engineering	905,200	1,140,000		
Residential care	745,700	1,171,000		
Child care	604,500	800,000		
Apparel manufacturing	547,100	650,000		
TV, radio, music stores	500,300	639,800		
Newspapers	442,500	401,000		
Beauty salons	410,500	465,000		
Non-store retailers	346,400	537,200		
Medical supplies	279,100	334,600		
Advertising	268,200	323,200		
Radio & TV broadcasting	246,900	253,000		
Railroad transportation	230,700	184,900		
Retail bakeries	206,400	247,700		
Personal credit	185,200	246,600		
Cable and pay TV	181,000	230,000		
Video tape rental	165,300	184,900		
Knitting mills	159,400	127,800		
Motion picture theaters	138,100	135,200		
Commercial sports	126,500	160,000		
Funeral services	99,400	110,100		
Museums and zoos	92,600	131,400		
Coal mining	91,600	59,400		
Luggage and leather	45,400	34,400		
Tobacco products	40,600	29,500		

Self-Assessment

The first step toward choosing a career that's right for you is to consider the things you like to do. Use the grid below to assess characteristics about yourself. Then check the next page to learn how you can score yourself on this exercise.

Directions: Place a check (√) in the shaded box next to each statement that describes something you like to do. If you don't enjoy an activity, leave the boxes blank.

I like to:	1	2	3	4	5	6
fix electrical things	☑					
play team sports			☑			
sketch, draw, paint						☑
keep accurate records		☑				
think abstractly					☑	
write factual reports					☑	
sell things or promote ideas			☑			
play a musical instrument	☑					
pitch a tent						☑
follow clearly defined procedures				☑		
plan and supervise an activity					☑	
be elected to office		☑				
solve math problems						☑
work with numbers and data				☑		
help people with problems			☑			
write stories and poems			☑			
attend concerts and art exhibits	☑					
work outdoors		☑				
use computers						☑
be responsible for details					☑	
make decisions that affect others			☑			
sing, act, and dance					☑	
meet important people	☑					
build things				☑		
lead a group discussion						☑
do a lot of paperwork		☑				
perform lab experiments			☑			
use a microscope			☑			
read fiction, plays, poetry					☑	
give talks or speeches					☑	
organize activities and events	☑					
be physically active				☑		
mediate disputes				☑		
teach or train others		☑				
work independently		☑				

So, what do your check marks mean? First, total the number of checks in each column, record them in this chart, and circle the top three. Then read the descriptions below:

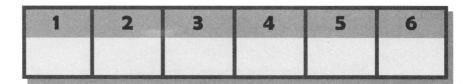

1	2	3	4	5	6

If one of your top three scores is in Box #1, you are interested in activities that require coordination or physical strength. You like to work with real problems instead of abstract ones. You're probably interested in scientific or mechanical areas.

If one of your top three score is in Box #2, you like to organize and understand things for yourself, but you're not interested in persuading others. You often enjoy working alone and are oriented more toward data and numbers than toward people.

If one of your top three scores is in Box #3, you value self-expression, dislike rigidity and structure, and are prone to be emotional. You are creative and artistic. You are probably interested in music, the fine arts, and crafts.

If one of your top three scores is in Box #4, you like to help people learn new things. You'd rather spend an evening talking with a friend than an afternoon playing basketball or skiing. You're a good listener and are interested in people. Friends often come to you for help in solving problems.

If one of your top three scores is in Box #5, you have keen verbal skills and like to use those skills to persuade others. You could probably be a good salesperson, advertiser, or politician.

If one of your top three scores is in Box #6, you don't mind rules and regulations, especially when you are in control. You enjoy order, and you like things organized. Messy things make you crazy. You are interested in tasks that require accuracy and precision.

Financial Fitness for Life: Shaping Up Your Financial Future Student Workouts, ©National Council on Economic Education

Judging from your responses, prioritize the career clusters below.
(Number 1 is the cluster that is most appealing; Number 6 is the least appealing.)

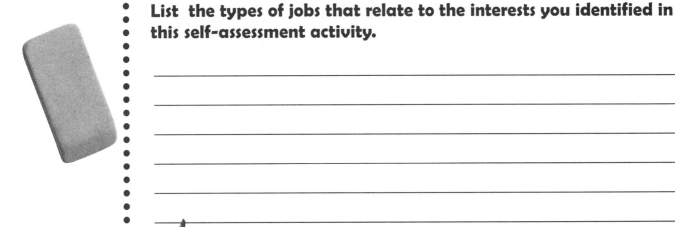

	Career Cluster	Typical jobs
_____	Arts and communication	Actor, dancer, newscaster, stagehand
_____	Business & technology	Accountant, banker, travel agent
_____	Engineering & industry	Mechanic, medical technician, plumber
_____	Environmental science	Botanist, florist, marine biologist
_____	Health services	Aerobics instructor, dentist, veterinarian
_____	Human services	Cook, detective, judge, teacher

List the types of jobs that relate to the interests you identified in this self-assessment activity.

Adapted from John Holland, PhD, "Holland Occupational Themes"
http://jobs.esc.state.nc.us/soicc/planning/cla.htm

Human Capital and SCANS on the Job

Read the job requirements on the next page, taken from actual classified job ads. Then check which ads require the SCANS skills listed below. Write the numbers of the ads in the blanks. (All blanks will have more than one ad listed.)

_____Basic skills (specific education requirements)

_____Interpersonal skills (getting along with people)

_____Teamwork

_____Ability to use technology

_____Good oral communication

_____Problem solving

_____Positive work ethic (good attitude)

_____Experience

_____Organizational skills

In the blanks below, write a short letter explaining why you should be considered for one of the jobs described in the ads. Be sure to include examples of how your human capital meets the requirements listed in the advertisement.

_____

_____

_____

_____

_____

_____

_____

_____

_____

34

Classified Advertisements

1 Computer Systems Administrator

Leading metal company seeks an individual to be responsible for all daily operations of our Windows Network, running 30 workstations and specialized software. Will develop documents, provide technical support, conduct training and assist in creating new forms and reports.

Must have good knowledge of software, Internet and computer basics. Excellent communication skills required; ability to learn/think independently.

Competitive benefits and salary.

5 BIOLOGIST

Manufacturer of medical lab supplies seeks biologists. Responsibilities include project testing, interpreting and reporting test results. You will investigate problems, recommend corrective actions and develop new methods for testing existing products.

Must possess a degree in Life Sciences and have 3 years experience. Computer experience recommended.

Competitive salary and benefits package.

9 GRAPHIC DESIGN SUPERVISOR

Exciting opportunity for a detail-oriented individual with excellent organizational and communication skills. Job will include managing production and projects.

Proficiency in Quark, Photoshop, and knowledge of Macintosh systems are a must.

Must be able to coordinate many projects at a time.

Benefits include medical and dental insurance, profit sharing, 401k, and 30% employee discount.

2 HOTEL Sales Manager

Prestigious hotel is looking for an energetic manager to join our winning sales team. You will be responsible for selling and servicing small meetings in a fast paced environment. The ideal candidate will have hotel background and be a highly motivated team player.

Excellent salary and benefits, including medical, dental and 401k.

6 Restaurant Manager

OCEANSIDE RESTAURANT IS SEARCHING FOR A MANAGER.

Minimum of 3 years experience in a luxury setting, excellent human relations and administrative skills. Must be able to accommodate guests in a gracious, sincere, timely and confident manner.

Superior benefits package including health, dental and life insurance, profit sharing and 401k.

8 NETWORK MANAGER

Health Care Provider seeks someone to drive the development of a health network. Responsibilities include maintaining existing network, resolving health insurance claims and educating patients about policies and procedures.

Must have a Master's Degree and 3 years experience. Strong communication skills are expected. Word and Excel proficiency required. Some travel.

Competitive salary, excellent benefits, ongoing opportunities for professional development.

3 Auto Sales

We're expanding our sales staff. We need motivated sales people with good communication skills and a team spirit.

We offer commissions, bonuses, flexible hours, paid vacation, medical and dental plan, 401k and opportunities for advancement.

4 Administrative Assistant

Help design your own position. New warehouse needs someone to take charge of the phones and run the office. Must enjoy making order out of chaos, beating deadlines and helping co-workers. PC skills, pleasant disposition, and good sense of humor are required.

Full time. Good salary and benefits.

7 EDITORIAL COORDINATOR

You'll coordinate a team of editors and proofreaders assigned to a variety of projects. Must be a problem solver with strong team skills. Effective verbal and written communication is essential. Other responsibilities may include checking research and making corrections. You'll also update files, edit and run reports.

PC and Mac experience a must. Excellent salary and benefits including 401k

10 Customer Service Representative

Manufacturer of bakeware seeks an experienced customer service rep. Candidate must have excellent phone skills, a positive attitude, and ability to solve problems on the spot. Must be proficient in Microsoft Word and have data entry experience.

Benefits include Medical/Dental/Vision Insurance, 401k plan and a fitness facility.

Financial Fitness for Life: Shaping Up Your Financial Future Student Workouts, ©National Council on Economic Education

EXERCISE 3.4

How Do Entrepreneurs Earn A Living?

You probably noticed that the job listings in Activity 3.3 included information about salaries and benefits. Most people like having the security of a regular salary, paid health care insurance, and a pension package. Entrepreneurs are different. When they take on the challenge of running their own businesses, they have to provide their own paychecks, insurance, and retirement plans. Consider the following situation.

Dimitrio's Furniture Shop

Dimitrio is an entrepreneur. He quit his job at a local furniture store to open his own business. Being a talented woodworker, he handcrafts some furniture to sell; he finds other items at auctions, repairs and resells them at a profit.

The figures below show how much Dimitrio earned each month when he worked as an employee at the furniture store. (For the sake of simplicity, taxes and social security are not included.)

Dimitrio's salary when he worked at the furniture store	$3,000.00
The value of Dimitrio's medical insurance	150.00
The value of Dimitrio's dental insurance	75.00
The value of Dimitrio's vision insurance	75.00
The amount Dimitrio's employer contributed to his retirement	60.00

The figures below show Dimitrio's July expenses in his new business.

Rent	$1,750.00
Electricity	230.00
Heat	320.00
Water	215.00
Advertising	1,200.00
Materials, supplies and equipment	22,400.00
Maintenance and service of equipment	350.00

Financial Fitness for Life: Shaping Up Your Financial Future Student Workouts, ©National Council on Economic Education

A Dimitrio had enough revenue in July to (1) pay his July expenses and (2) pay himself the same monthly salary and benefits he earned when he worked for someone else. How much revenue did Dimitrio earn in July?

_____

B If Dimitrio made the same amount of total salary and benefits running his own business as when he worked for someone else, should Dimitrio continue to run his own business?

_____

About what percent of total revenue did Dimitrio use to pay himself in July?

_____

BONUS

37

ASSESSMENT

3.1

What's Wrong With This Picture?

Read the story below, and underline every statement that illustrates habits that will **NOT** prepare Kelly for a successful career. Then, above each incorrect statement, write the letter of the SCANS skill that Kelly is lacking.

HINT: You should find more than 12 mistakes.

Choose from these SCANS skills:

A Reading, writing and math

B Interpersonal skills

C Teamwork

D Use of technology

E Oral communication

F Problem solving

G Good work ethic/on time/good attitude

H Organizational skills

Kelly is a seventh grader at Middleton Middle School. Her first class begins at 8:05, so she sets her alarm for 7:30. That way she's out of the kitchen door at 7:50 and ready for her 20-minute walk to school. Yesterday, when she entered the building, she saw the principal, Ms. Ramirez.

"Yo," Kelly shouted. "What's happenin'?"

"You're late, Kelly," said the principal, frowning.

"Whatever!" replied Kelly, as she raced down the hall.

In class, Kelly ruffled through her book bag but could not find any pens, pencils, or paper. When Mr. Choy asked for her math assignment, she didn't have that either.

"You'll have to go to the office," Mr. Choy told her.

In the principal's office, Kelly was asked to answer the phone while one of the secretaries stepped out. When the phone rang, Kelly picked it up.

- "Hey, man, this is Middleton school. Whaddya want?" she said.

- The caller hung up, but Kelly could not figure out why. She decided to leave a note for the secretary. It said: "Deer Sekretery, Somebody called and hung up. I dont no who it was."

- When the phone rang again, Kelly said, "Whooze zis?"

- "Please have Ms. Ramirez call the superintendent's office by 9:30."

- "Okay, okay," said Kelly. On a piece of scrap paper she wrote: "Ms. Ramirez—go to the custodian's office after 9:30."

- "Kelly, you need to keep a good record of the calls," said the school clerk.

- "You can't tell me what to do," shouted Kelly. "I'm doin' ya a favor by helpin' ya out."

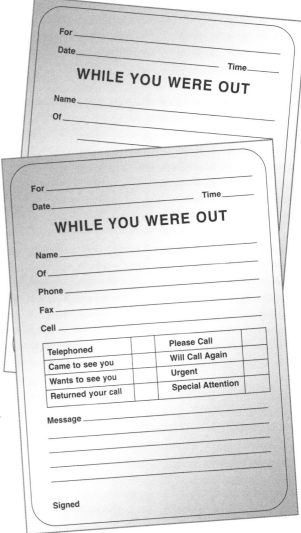

The next day when Kelly woke up, it was dark in her bedroom. She flipped the switch about ten times, but her lamp would not light.

"Hey, what's wrong with my lamp?" she yelled to her mother.

"Maybe the bulb burned out," her mother suggested.

"Oh, I never thought of that," said Kelly.

Kelly had not done her homework, so she decided not to go to school. "Let's see, that's 15 days absent so far this year. That ain't too bad," she said.

When Kelly finally returned to school her social studies teacher, Ms. Musielewicz, sent her to the computer lab to do some research for a big project. In the lab, Kelly was clueless. She did not even know how to turn on the computer. The lab assistant tried to help her, but Kelly just shrugged.

"I took that stupid computer class last year, but I didn't like it. Besides, I'm gonna be a mechanic when I'm done with school. I don't need no computer skills."

Financial Fitness for Life: Shaping Up Your Financial Future Student Workouts, ©National Council on Economic Education

Finally, it was the last period of the day—gym class. The substitute teacher was assigning the students to teams for basketball. When Kelly got the ball, she dribbled down the floor and tried to shoot, even though she was surrounded by players from the other team.

"Pass. Pass the ball!" shouted the teacher.

But Kelly just tried to shoot again and was blocked by another player. Every time she got the ball, Kelly tried to shoot. She never passed to another player.

When the bell rang at the end of the day, Kelly grabbed her book bag and ran out of the building. On the way home she stopped at the store and bought a candy bar for $0.55, giving the clerk a one-dollar bill.

"With tax, that's 59 cents. Your change is 41 cents," the cashier said, handing Kelly a quarter, a nickel and a penny.

"Hey," said another shopper. "That's not the right change."

"Sure it is," shrugged Kelly. "It must be. The man said it was."

When Kelly got home, her mother asked how things went at school.

"All right, I guess," she replied. "But I can't wait to finish and get a job. Then I can do anything I want."

Give Kelly some advice for how to improve her human capital and increase her chances for a successful career.

_____

_____

_____

_____

_____

_____

_____

_____

_____

_____

_____

Financial Fitness for Life: Shaping Up Your Financial Future Student Workouts, ©National Council on Economic Education

LESSON 4
Productivity

Warm-Up

If you live in a city, you probably don't often think about the big changes that have taken place on U.S. farms. For example:

▲ In 1960, the average U.S. corn farmer was able to harvest 60 bushels of corn from an acre of land. Today, that number has increased to 120 bushels.

▲ Wheat yields have also doubled, from 19 bushels per acre in 1960 to 38 bushels today.

▲ Soybeans have increased from 24 bushels per acre to 34.

▲ Cattle have gotten bigger too. In the 1960's, beef cattle weighed an average of 360 pounds; now the average is 569 pounds.

Source: www.purdue.edu/UNS/
html4ever/9703.Martin.productivity.html

MUSCLE DEVELOPERS

Learn these ideas, practice them, and develop your financial fitness muscles.

✔ Productivity relates to the output of resources, such as how much a worker produces each day.

✔ Improvements in capital resources lead to greater productivity.

✔ Investment in human capital leads to greater productivity.

✔ Increased productivity results in a higher standard of living.

Technology has affected every area of productive resources. Productive resources are natural (soil, climate, minerals), human (workers skills and knowledge), and capital (buildings, machinery and tools).

Look at how technology and education have affected productive resources:

Natural resources. Fertilizers, herbicides and insecticides, irrigation and crop rotation have increased the yield per acre of land.

Human resources. Farmers are educated today to use techniques and equipment that were unknown 100 years ago.

Capital resources. High-tech tools and machinery increase the output that farmers can expect from their fields and herds.

41

All these improvements mean more products for consumers: more steaks, hot-dogs, pizzas, and, yes, more broccoli too. Increased productivity means that our standard of living is higher.

What does this have to do with the millions of people who don't live on farms? And what does it have to do with you?

Technology has not only affected farmers. Think about how your life has changed in the past few years because of new and improved tools. You can type a report quicker on a computer than on a typewriter; you can do research on the Internet at home without having to go to the library; you can order books and music CDs online instead of driving all the way to the mall.

That makes you more productive: you can accomplish the same amount of work in less time and with less effort. Someday you'll be able to use your new productivity and your improved human capital to get a better job, earn a higher income, and enjoy a higher standard of living for yourself and your family.

FITNESS VOCABULARY

Productivity – The amount of output per unit of input; e.g., if 5 workers can produce 25 gizmos in one day, the productivity per day is 5 gizmos per worker.

Productive resources – Natural, human, and capital resources.

Natural resources – Gifts of nature, such as land, water, and air.

Human resources – Everyone in the economy who works; includes the entrepreneur who puts resources together to produce new goods and services.

Capital resources – Tools, machines, and other devices that make work faster, easier, and more efficient.

Showing Your Strength

If you know the answers to these questions, you are developing some financial muscle.

1 **How can productivity be increased?** *(Productivity can be increased by improving any of the resources. If land [natural resources] can be improved by adding fertilizer or a new technology, land will produce more crops. If workers or entrepreneurs use improved work procedures, they will produce more goods or services. More or improved equipment can result in increased production.)*

2   **What are some examples of natural resources?** *(Air, land, water, trees, and minerals are natural resources.)*

3   **What are capital resources?** *(One definition is "goods that are used to make other goods." Capital resources include buildings, bulldozers, trucks, pencils, computers, hammers, cash registers, and other devices that make work more efficient.)*

4   **How do human resources affect productivity?** *(The quality of an economy's human resources is one of the key reasons for its productivity. A skilled and educated workforce, both entrepreneurs and workers, is able to use capital and natural resources to produce a variety of goods and services.)*

5   **Why is it important to invest in your own human capital?** *(By increasing your skills, knowledge, and experience, you become a more valuable worker and may earn a higher income.)*

6   **What is the relationship between productivity and standard of living?** *(There is a direct relationship between the two. The higher the productivity, the higher the standard of living. Usually high productivity means there are more goods and services available and more income to buy those items.)*

Financial Fitness for Life: Shaping Up Your Financial Future Student Workouts, ©National Council on Economic Education

The Whole Story

A **couple of years ago, Mike and Chris started a summer business. It all started in February when the guys were talking about how they might earn some money. They were both 12, so they knew getting a job in a store or fast food place was out of the question because of their age. They decided to go into business for themselves. After examining all of the types of work typically done by boys their age, they decided to go into the grass-mowing business.**

Chris went to work immediately. February and March are too early to cut grass, but he knew it wasn't too soon to start lining up customers. He printed flyers and went for long, neighborhood walks, placing the flyers on the doorknob of every house he saw. He hung flyers on signs and trees. He placed ads in local papers and on bulletin boards at all the local stores.

When summer arrived, Mike and Chris had enough work to keep them busy 20 hours a week.

They cut grass all around the neighborhood. Chris even contacted Yolanda, the owner of the neighborhood ball fields, and arranged to cut the fields every Wednesday morning. The ball field was a good account; Chris had negotiated with Yolanda to get a fee of $16.00 per hour ($8.00 per person).

Week after week, Mike and Chris cut the grass at the ball field. They had identical lawn mowers, began cutting at the same time, and finished in two hours. However, at the end of each two-hour work session, Mike had cut three-fourths of the field while Chris had cut only one-fourth. Yolanda commended Mike for his productivity.

It may have been that Mike was simply a better worker than Chris was; however, there may have been other differences that affected the boys' productivity.

Financial Fitness for Life: Shaping Up Your Financial Future Student Workouts, ©National Council on Economic Education

A What skills did Chris have that Mike may not have?

B Was Mike really more productive than Chris was?

Answer questions (A) and (B) on the lines below:

_____

_____

_____

_____

_____

_____

_____

_____

_____

_____

_____

_____

_____

ASSESSMENT

4.1

Career Search

Choose a career that interests you.

For example, you might be curious about a career in web design, biological research, public relations, or health care. Even though your first full-time job may seem a long way off, it's never too early to begin to prepare. Find two articles from a popular magazine, a web site, or newspaper that features a career that interests you. You may substitute an interview with someone currently in your career choice for one of the articles. Use the information in the articles and interview to answer the following questions. Attach a copy of the articles or interview to this sheet.

On what career are you focusing?

_____

What do you find interesting about this career?

_____

_____

What capital resources might someone use in this career?

_____

_____

In what ways do the use of these capital resources help the worker to be more productive?

_____

_____

_____

_____

What skills are required of someone in this career?

_____

_____

What level of education would you need to acquire the skills for this career?

_____

What subjects, in particular, would you need to study?

_____

_____

What is the average annual salary for someone in this career?

_____

LESSON 5
Why Stay in School?

Warm-Up

Question: *Why do people work?*
Answer: *To make money.*

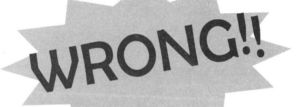

WRONG!!

People do not work for money, but rather for the goods, services, and security that money can buy. Of course, you'll be able to buy more of the things you want if you have more money. Besides working for the things money can buy, people also work for the personal satisfaction they gain from the work.

You can acquire money in several different ways. You could steal it—but that harms other people, and living in prison isn't too much fun. You can receive it as a gift—but that's not too steady or predictable. (Besides, your Aunt Mabel isn't going to send you a birthday check for the rest of your life.) If you're like most people, you'll get most of your money by working for it.

Working is something you'll probably do for 30, 40, or 50 years. So how can you make the most of your time on the job? The best thing to do is to plan ahead and invest in your human capital by getting as much education and

48

FITNESS VOCABULARY

Income – Money earned during a specified period (e.g., $10 per hour or $50,000 per year.)

Opportunity cost – The next-best alternative that is given up when a choice is made.

Trade off – Giving up a little of something in order to get a little more of something else.

Human capital – Knowledge, skills, and experiences that make a worker more productive.

Wages – Income earned from working.

training as possible, especially in a field in which you have an interest or aptitude. By staying in school, learning a trade, earning an advanced degree, or serving an apprenticeship, you can master the skills and gain the knowledge you'll need to be successful in a career that you enjoy. Studies show that people with more education have more job satisfaction and earn higher incomes.

If you choose to stay in school you'll learn extra skills, become a more valuable worker, and have the opportunity to earn a higher income. With a higher income you'll have more opportunities to use the money you earn to plan for your financial future.

Showing Your Strength

If you know the answers to these questions, you are developing some financial muscle.

1 **Why do people with more education earn higher incomes?** *(Education is a way of investing in human capital and acquiring more skills, knowledge, and experience. The added knowledge makes you a more valuable worker. Employers are willing to pay more for more valuable workers.)*

2 **Does everyone with more education earn more?** *(Sometimes people with less education earn a lot of money, but that's because they possess certain skills and knowledge that are in great demand. For example, some professional baseball players do not have college degrees, but they have a specialized skill that many other people do not have.)*

49

3 **What about entrepreneurs? Do they all have advanced degrees?** *(Entrepreneurs do not all have advanced degrees, but many do. However, they are often innovators who have a specialized kind of human capital. They possess skills and creativity that others do not have. By using their human capital in their own businesses, entrepreneurs become valuable in the marketplace.)*

4 **What's the best way to increase the likelihood of earning a higher income in the future?** *(Studies indicate a positive relationship between more education and higher income, so the best thing to do is stay in school and get all the education and training you can.)*

MUSCLE DEVELOPERS

Learn these ideas, practice them, and develop your financial fitness muscles.

✔ People can earn income by working for others or by working for themselves. People who work for themselves are called entrepreneurs. They develop an idea and create goods or services that other people buy.

✔ Investing in your human capital can make you a more valuable and highly paid worker.

✔ Choosing to invest in your human capital involves an opportunity cost. (For example, when you choose to stay in school you give up the income you could have earned if you were working.)

✔ Investing in human capital may involve a trade-off. You might choose to go to school only part-time so you can continue to work part-time, or so that you can spend more time with your friends or family.

✔ People who have more education and training generally earn higher incomes than those who have less education and training.

EXERCISE 5.1

Some Things About School Are So...

Finish the sentence "Some things about school are so...," by listing those things about school you think are difficult or hard, those that are comfortable or so-so, and those that are easy for you.

Difficult	Comfortable	Easy

What actions can you take to improve your ability and skill in areas you find difficult?

_____

_____

_____

What is your plan of action, your timeline, for improvement?

_____

_____

_____

51

EXERCISE 5.2

Steps to Success

Median earnings of full-time wage and salary workers

Advanced Degree
$54,600

Bachelor's Degree
$42,796

Associate's Degree
$30,940

High School Diploma
$26,208

High School Drop Out
$18,876

Median means that half of the people in the category earn less than (and half earn more than) the number given.

Source: http://stats.bls.gov: Table 4 Quintiles and selected deciles of usual annual earnings of full-time wage and salary workers by selected characteristics, second quarter 2000 averages.

Instructions: Study the table and answer the questions that follow.

52

1 Calculate the difference in salary between

a. a high school dropout and a high school graduate. _____

b. a high school graduate and a graduate from
a two-year college program (associate's degree). _____

c. a two-year college graduate and a four-year
college graduate (bachelor's degree). _____

d. a four-year college graduate and an individual
with an advanced degree (master's or doctorate). _____

2 Calculate the lifetime earnings of each level of educational attainment using the table below. Have students assume each person works until 70 years of age.

Other assumptions include:

a. the high school dropout begins full-time work at age 16.

b. the high school graduate begins full-time work at age 18.

c. the graduate of the two-year college begins full-time work at age 20.

d. the graduate of the four-year college begins full-time work at age 22.

e. the graduate with a master's degree begins full-time work at age 24.

	H.S. dropout	H.S. diploma	Associate's degree	Bachelor's degree	Advanced degree
Annual Income	$18,876	$26,208	$30,940	$42,796	$54,600
Years worked					
Life earnings					

53

THEME

3

Tomorrow's Money: Getting to the End of the Rainbow
(Saving)

Bank of America deposit slip graphic with the following visible text:

Bank of America

☐ Checking ☐ Savings Deposit - NC **CREDIT**

Please Check Proper Box.
All items received subject to terms and conditions of applicable laws, regulations and deposit agreement.

Date

Name and Address

Save time in line and help us avoid errors. The next time you make a deposit, please use your pre-printed deposit slips for your account.

Telephone No. (   )

Sign here if cash received

Proper identification required when using this document.

For NC Use Only

33-14-3074B 7-1999

Cash
Currency
Coin

Checks

Sub Total

Less Cash Received

Total Deposit

$

⑈540560136⑈

Introduction

If you could have a wish list, what would it include? A mega stereo system? A new wardrobe? A computer? All of the above?

Wouldn't it be great to have all the money you needed right now to buy all the things you want?

Chances are, though, you can't afford all the things on your wish list. That's why you have to make choices. One choice might be simply to do without one of the items, perhaps the stereo system. Another choice, though, could be to save part of your income for a period of time until you have enough to pay for the stereo. This might take a few weeks or months, or maybe even a year, but by choosing to give up spending now in order to save for the future, you would be able to buy that stereo eventually.

LESSON 6
Why Save?

In order to be successful at saving so that they can buy the things they want most, people usually set goals. Those who stick with their goals find satisfaction in two ways. They get more of the goods and services they want most. They also feel a lot of self-satisfaction and a sense of accomplishment—like the feeling a sprinter gets who wins a big race, or like a student who gets an A on a difficult test.

This lesson introduces you to the importance of setting saving goals and investing for the future. Some goals may be achieved quickly; others will take longer. The good news is: if you consider your options carefully, you'll probably make the right decisions, decisions that can help you reach the goals you have set.

MUSCLE DEVELOPERS

Learn these ideas, practice them, and develop your financial fitness muscles.

✔ Saving can help you get the things you want most.

✔ Saving goals can be short-, medium- or long-term, depending on what you're saving for and how much you can save each period (week, month or year).

✔ When you save for the future, you give up the chance to spend now.

✔ The best spending alternative you give up when you save is your opportunity cost.

✔ Because resources are scarce, you have to make choices.

✔ People choose to save and invest so that they can have the things they want in the future.

No matter how little or how much money you want to save, you'll have to give up buying something now in order to save and invest for the future. The thing you give up is your *opportunity cost*.

If you save your loose change until you have a dollar to buy a large candy bar, you might be giving up the opportunity to buy gum from the gum ball machine now and then. In that case, the gum balls are your opportunity cost. If you save $10 a month for six months until you have $60 for a concert ticket, you might give up the chance to spend money at an amusement park one month, buy a music CD the next month, or treat your brother to a pizza the third month. In every case, the best spending alternative you give up when you decide to save is your opportunity cost.

You may find it difficult to imagine saving for five or six years to buy something you really want. That's a long time when you're 12 or 13. In fact, it's nearly half your life! But lots of people set long-term goals for themselves. They plan for things that are three, five, or even ten years in the future.

FITNESS VOCABULARY

Short-term goals – Goals you plan to achieve in fewer than two months.

Medium-term goals – Goals you plan to achieve in two months to three years.

Long-term goals – Goals you plan to achieve in more than three years.

Opportunity cost – The value of the next-best alternative given up when a choice is made.

Scarcity – The economic problem that exists because of unlimited wants and limited resources.

Saving – The act of putting something aside for later use.

Investing – Saving money in order to earn a financial return.

Showing Your Strength

If you know the answers to these questions, you are developing some financial muscle.

1 **Why is it important to set goals?** *(Goals are end points that act as incentives. They help you stay focused on saving so you can buy the things you want most.)*

2 **When should you set short-, medium-, or long-term savings goals?** *(Set a short-term savings goal if you think it will take you fewer than two months to save enough money. Set a medium-term saving goal for one between two months and three years. If you need to save for more than three years, set a long-term goal.)*

3 **What is the opportunity cost of saving?** *(Saving for some future goal means giving up the chance to spend now. Postponing consumption allows people to save for the purchase of future goods and services.)*

4 **What is the difference between saving and investing?** *(Saving is the act of setting something aside. You can save sea shells, rocks, pennies or even dollar bills in a jar at home. Investing means earning a financial return. Putting money in a bank savings account, bond, or stock is investing. Your intent is to earn a return on your money.)*

57

EXERCISE
6.1

How To Reach a Goal

Read the stories below and calculate whether students at Elm Valley Middle School can reach their goals. Identify whether the goals are short- (up to two months), medium- (two months to three years), or long-term (more than three years). If any of the students in the stories cannot reach his or her goal, suggest some ways he or she could reach the saving goal.

1 José tutors some sixth graders in math and earns $36 a week. He always puts $15 in his college fund and uses the rest for everyday expenses.

At a jewelry store downtown, he spotted a bracelet that he'd like to buy for his mother's 40th birthday, three years from now. It was a real beauty, but the price was $2,100. If José puts aside $15 a week for college and spends $8 a week on himself, how long will it take him to save enough to buy the bracelet? (Do not consider any interest he might be earning on his savings.) Will it be a short-, medium- or long-term goal? Explain why. If he cannot save enough according to the present schedule, suggest some ways he could reach the goal.

_____

_____

_____

_____

_____

2 Lauren earns $17 every Saturday baby-sitting for her neighbors. She also receives an allowance of $10 per week for the chores she regularly does at home. Her parents have a rule that she must put half of her allowance in her college fund, a savings account from which she never withdraws any money.

Lauren plays tenor saxophone in the school band and has been renting an instrument from the music department. Last week Lauren saw a used sax at a music store in the mall. She'd really like to buy it, but it costs $175. Her parents told her that if she saves the $175, they'd pay the sales tax for her.

If Lauren continues to contribute to her college fund, saves every penny she earns, including her allowance, how long will it take her to save enough to buy the sax? Will it be a short-, medium-, or long-term goal? Explain why. If she cannot save enough according to the present schedule, suggest some ways she could reach the goal.

_____

_____

_____

_____

3 Darnell works in his father's office on Mondays, Wednesdays, and Fridays and earns $75 a week. He saves $20 a week in his college fund, gives $5 a week to charity, and spends $8 a week on snacks and entertainment.

Recently Darnell became interested in golf, and he wants to become a better player. Golf lessons at a local park cost $300 and begin in six weeks. Is this a short-, medium–, or long-term goal? If Darnell continues his saving, spending and sharing habits, will he be able to save enough money in time to attend the first lesson? Explain why. If not, what could he change?

_____

_____

_____

_____

59

EXERCISE

6.2

Rolling for a Goal: A Game for Two or More Players

This game involves setting a saving goal, and trying to meet it. Two or more people can play the game. Before starting the game, the teacher will provide the game cards. Shuffle them and place them in a pile. You will need two dice, pencil, paper, and the score sheet on the next page. Choose a person to go first.

1 Draw a card from the pile. This is your saving goal. Write this amount on line A of the score sheet.

2 Throw one die and multiply the number on the die by $10. Write this amount as the amount you can save each month on line B.

3 Calculate how many months you'll have to save in order to reach your goal, and write the answer on line C. (line A 4 line B)

4 Identify the goal as either short- (S), medium- (M), or long-term (L) and write on line D.

5 Roll two dice and multiply the two numbers to determine the number of months during which you will be able to save. Enter that number on line E.

6 Will you be able to reach your goal? Compare the number on line E with the one on line C. If E is greater than or equal to C, give yourself 2 points on line F; if not, give yourself 0 points on line F.

7 Play four rounds. Add the numbers in Column F. The person with the most points wins. If winning scores are tied, those players can play additional rounds until there is one winner.

60

Score Sheet for
Rolling for a Goal

	Game #1	Game #2	Game #3	Game #4
A Saving goal				
B Amount saved each month ($10 x roll of one die).				
C Number of months needed to meet goal (A÷B).				
D Short- (S), Medium- (M), or Long-term goal (L).				
E Number of months you will be able to save. (Roll of two dice multiplied together.)				
F Yes, I will be able to meet my saving goal. (Give yourself 2 points.) No, I will not be able to meet my saving goal. (0 points.)				
Totals				

ASSESSMENT

6.1

Short-, Medium-, and Long-Term Goals

The chart below shows how much money six people want to save. Each person is able to save a different amount each month. Calculate how long each person must save to reach his/her goal. Then indicate by writing S, M, or L, if it is a short-, medium-, or long-term goal.

Person	Amount to be Saved	Amount Saved Each Month	How Many Months	How Many Years	Short-, Medium-, or Long-Term
Abby	$ 780.00	$20.00			
Ben	25.00	15.00			
Cherise	700.00	35.00			
Danuka	800.00	70.00			
Emilio	90.00	50.00			
Festis	2,900.00	75.00			

Complete the following exercise about Cherise based on what you calculated in the above grid.

Cherise saves $35 every month. It will take her _____ months to reach her saving goal of $700. During those months, she could be spending her money, but instead she sticks to her saving plan. That means that every month she gives up some goods or service that she could have bought with the $35 she is saving.

Financial Fitness for Life: Shaping Up Your Financial Future Student Workouts, ©National Council on Economic Education

In the blanks below, list the opportunity costs Cherise might incur during the months she saves toward her goal. (Be creative. Think of opportunity costs that could be associated with the months. For example, in April her opportunity cost might be a new raincoat for April showers).

Month	Opportunity Cost	Explanation
January	_____	_____ _____
February	_____	_____ _____
March	_____	_____ _____
April	_____	_____ _____
May	_____	_____ _____
June	_____	_____ _____
July	_____	_____ _____
August	_____	_____ _____
September	_____	_____ _____
October	_____	_____ _____
November	_____	_____ _____
December	_____	_____ _____

Financial Fitness for Life: Shaping Up Your Financial Future Student Workouts, ©National Council on Economic Education

LESSON 7
Types of Savings Plans

Warm-Up

If you saved $100 under your mattress, in 50 years you'd still have $100, right?

Well, yes and no. Even though you would still have $100 in your hand, you couldn't buy as much now as you could have bought 50 years ago, because things tend to get more expensive over time. After all, back in the 1950s you could see a movie for a quarter, and the price of a phone call was only five cents. Now things cost more. That's called *inflation*: a general increase in the prices of goods and services. In order to "keep up with inflation," people don't save their money under a mattress. They have a number of different options when it comes to saving. One option is a bank or another savings institution.

Most financial institutions offer a number of ways to save and to earn interest. In this lesson you will learn about some of them: regular savings accounts, money market deposit accounts, certificates of deposit (CDs), and United States Savings Bonds. All these savings plans offer safety and liquidity for your money, and they pay you interest, too. In addition, each has its own advantages and disadvantages. It's important to understand all the pros and cons when you choose where to save your money.

FITNESS VOCABULARY

Statement savings account – an interest-bearing account that can be opened with a small amount of money; funds can easily be deposited or withdrawn.

Money market account – an interest-bearing account that may require higher minimum balances than regular accounts. Deposits can be added at any time, but withdrawals may be limited without paying a penalty.

Certificate of deposit (CD) – an interest-bearing account that requires a higher minimum deposit and a higher minimum balance than regular accounts and has a specific time limit (6 months, 1 year, 5 years, etc.). If deposits are withdrawn before the specified time, there is a penalty.

United States Savings Bond – technically, a loan to the U.S. government upon which you earn interest. There are two major types of U.S. Savings Bonds. One kind (Series EE) can be purchased for half their face value; for example, a $100 bond costs $50. When the bonds mature they can be redeemed at face value. Another kind (Series I) is sold at its face value, (you would pay $100 for a $100 bond,) and earns interest over the time it is held.

Opportunity cost – the next-best alternative that is given up when a choice is made.

Inflation – a general increase in the prices of goods and services.

Learn these ideas, practice them, and develop your financial fitness muscles.

MUSCLE DEVELOPERS

✔ Saving can help you get the things you want most.

✔ Because a savings account earns interest, it can help you keep pace with inflation.

✔ The U.S. government insures money in a regular savings account in most financial institutions. Your money is safe and secure, and it earns interest.

✔ Savers need to examine carefully the advantages and disadvantages of different savings options.

✔ Some options are better at different stages in your life.

✔ Many people make a habit of buying U.S. Savings Bonds. In fact, a lot of businesses offer a "payroll savings plan" that deducts a certain amount from every paycheck for the worker to automatically buy bonds.

✔ If you "cash in" a series EE bond before its maturity date, it will be worth less than its face value. You can find out how much a U.S. Savings Bond is worth by going to this web site: www.SAVINGSBONDS.GOV

✔ When you decide to save for the future, you have to give up some spending in the present. The thing you give up is your opportunity cost.

✔ Because of inflation, most goods and services cost more now than they did 50 or even 10 years ago. Inflation is usually expressed as a percentage. For example, if the inflation rate is 10% a year, a product that cost $100 last year will cost $110 this year. By saving money in interest-bearing accounts, the bad effects of inflation can be reduced.

Showing Your Strength

If you know the answers to these questions, you are developing some financial muscles.

1 **What are the differences and similarities between a regular savings account and a CD?** *(Both are ways to save, and the U.S. government insures both, so they are very safe and secure. However, a regular savings account allows deposits and withdrawals at any time. A CD has a higher interest rate but has a time limit; if you want to withdraw money ahead of time, you will lose some of the earned interest.)*

2 **What's the opportunity cost of buying a $100 U.S. Savings Bond?** *(A $100 Series EE bond costs $50, so the opportunity cost is the next best alternative you could have bought for $50 instead of buying the bond.)*

Types of Guaranteed Savings Instruments

All of the savings methods described here are guaranteed in most commercial banks, savings and loan associations, savings banks, and credit unions. This means you will not lose the money you have deposited. The U.S. federal government guarantees an individual's deposits up to $100,000 per banking institution through the Federal Deposit Insurance Corporation (FDIC). The National Credit Union Association (NCUA) has the same type of insurance for credit unions that the FDIC has for the other three institutions. The U.S. Savings Bonds are not guaranteed by any insurance; bonds are debts of the U.S. Treasury. The federal government, though, stands behind the payment of these debts so they are quite safe.

Savings Accounts

This is a traditional way to save money in a bank. As long as you keep money in your account, the bank pays you interest and your money grows. The most common kind of savings account is a **statement savings account**. For this account, the bank sends you a statement that details all of your deposits and withdrawals and the interest you've earned either once a month or once a quarter (every three months). Interest rates are usually lower than rates for other types of savings choices, but you can open an account with very little money. You can also withdraw your money whenever you like.

 Savings Account **Advantages**

▲ Your money is easy to access; you do not have to leave it in the bank for a specific amount of time. You can withdraw it without any penalty.

▲ The interest rate paid on the deposit can increase as general interest rates increase.

▲ You can open the account with a small amount of money.

 ### Savings Account **Disadvantages**

▲ Traditional savings accounts pay lower interest rates than other saving plans.
▲ Interest rates can go down as general interest rates go down.
▲ The bank may charge a service fee if the account balance is below a certain minimum.

Certificates of Deposit

The Certificate of Deposit, also known as a CD, is a specific amount of money that you deposit in the bank for a specific amount of time. The time period may be 6 months to several years, and the interest rate you get is unchanged for that time. For example, you might put $500 in a CD for six months or one year. Generally, the longer the time you agree to, the higher the interest rate. If you withdraw the money before the agreed time, you lose some of the interest you have earned.

 ### CD **Advantages**

▲ Banks pay higher interest for money invested in CDs than they do on traditional savings accounts at the time the CD is issued. Bankers know you probably will not withdraw your money for the agreed upon amount of time because of the penalty (lost interest) if you do.
▲ The locked-in interest rate can be advantageous if general interest rates go down during the time period of the CD.

 ### CD **Disadvantages**

▲ You will pay a substantial penalty if you withdraw your money early.
▲ The locked-in interest rate can be disadvantageous if interest rates increase during the time period of the CD.
▲ Generally, a minimum, such as $500, is required to open a CD.

Money Market Deposit Account

Money market deposit accounts are similar to checking accounts, because you can write checks on money market deposit accounts. They are insured through the Federal Deposit Insurance Corporation, a government agency. Do not confuse money market *deposit* accounts with money market accounts (notice that the word "deposit" is missing from the latter.) Money market accounts contain investments that are not insured by the FDIC. Many of these are offered by a brokerage firm.

Financial Fitness for Life: Shaping Up Your Financial Future Student Workouts, ©National Council on Economic Education

An increasing number of money market deposit accounts are combined with a statement checking account. The interest paid on these accounts could be less than a statement savings account, especially when there is no limitation on the number of checks written. In other cases, the interest rate may be higher than what is found on statement savings accounts. It varies from one financial institution to another.

 ## Money Market Deposit Account **Advantages**

▲ Money market deposit accounts allow periodic withdrawals, just like traditional savings accounts, with no penalty. It is very convenient to be able to write a check to withdraw money from this kind of savings account.

▲ Interest paid on savings increases as the general interest rate for credit increases.

▲ Money market deposit accounts may pay a higher rate of interest than regular savings accounts.

 ## Money Market Deposit Account **Disadvantages**

▲ Money market accounts require a significant minimum balance, often $1,000 or higher.

▲ The number of checks you can write without extra charges may be very limited.

▲ The interest rate goes down as the general interest rate goes down.

▲ The interest rate may be lower than a savings account.

United States Savings Bonds

Savings bonds are debt instruments (loans) issued by the United States Government. The person who buys the bond is the lender and the government is the borrower. Some savings bonds (Series EE) are purchased for one-half their face value and are later cashed at face value. Others (Series I) are purchased at face value.

 ## U.S. Savings Bonds **Advantages**

▲ Savings bonds can be purchased for as little as $25 (a $50 series EE bond).

▲ Savings bonds generally pay a higher rate of interest than a savings account.

▲ Interest rates increase as the general interest rate increases.

▲ Savers may not have to pay state and local income taxes on interest earned on government savings bonds.

▲ Parents who use savings bonds for their child's college education also enjoy a tax advantage.

U.S. Savings Bonds **Disadvantages**

▲ There can be a penalty for withdrawal of money from the bonds before maturity. The penalty varies with the type of U. S. Savings Bond that is purchased and when it is redeemed. This means the saver will lose a certain amount of interest already earned.

▲ Interest rates of a savings bond can go down if general interest rates go down.

After you have read all about savings instruments, decide where you should put your savings in the following situations:

1 You have savings of $100 that you may need within two months.

_____

2 You have savings of $1,000 that you may need within three years.

_____

3 You have savings of $1,000 that you may need within three months.

_____

4 You have savings of $10,000 but you wish to make periodic withdrawals.

_____

5 You have savings of $1,000 that you will need in three years. You believe the interest rate will be decreasing in the next couple of years.

_____

_____

6 A couple receives $2,000 from family members on the birth of their baby. The parents want to put it toward their newborn's college education.

_____

_____

EXERCISE 7.2

Savings Plans in My Community

Saving instrument	Minimum balance or deposit	Interest rate	Penalty for withdrawal	Fees
Statement savings account				
6-month CD				
12-month CD				
24-month CD				
Money market deposit account				
U.S. Savings Bond Series EE				
U.S. Savings Bond Series I				

Name of bank or institution _____

_____

Where did you get this information? *(For example, an interview of a bank representative, from the internet, or from a newspaper.)*

_____

_____

Are any of the accounts insured or bonds insured? If so, by whom and up to what amount?

_____

_____

_____

_____

70

Types of Savings Plans

Match the best savings plan with the situation.

Options:

A Savings account

B Certificate of deposit

C Money market deposit account

D U.S. Savings Bond

Situations:

1 _____ Alfredo has $100 and wants to be able to withdraw it at any time without penalty.

2 _____ Willie is eight years old and wants to save the $25 he received for his birthday for college.

3 _____ Juanita is in college. She just inherited $5000 from Aunt Mildred. She will need it for college expenses beginning in two months.

4 _____ Garth has $10,000 in savings that he will not need for a while. He believes interest rates will be going down in the next year.

5 _____ Kari has $2000 in savings. She wants to earn the most interest possible before she needs it for college in five years. She believes that interest rates will increase in the next few years.

Financial Fitness for Life: Shaping Up Your Financial Future Student Workouts, ©National Council on Economic Education

LESSON 8
Who Pays and Who Receives?

Warm-Up

A wise person once said, "You can work for your money, or you can let your money work for you." You work for your money when you get a job and begin to earn regular paychecks. Your money works for you when you save and invest it wisely.

Investing is a good idea because the money you save earns interest. Did you ever stop to think about how much interest you can earn on your savings?

In this lesson you will learn about saving, and about the effects of *simple and compound interest* on your investment. You'll use a quick formula, called *The Rule of 72*, to calculate how long it takes to double your money. Finally, you will find out that three things affect how hard your money can work for you:

▲ the amount you save
▲ the rate of interest
▲ the length of time you leave money in an account

As strange as it may seem, banks are businesses—just as grocery stores, gas stations and theaters are businesses. Every business wants to please its customers and earn a profit. Without a profit, a company will lose money and have to shut down.

Banks earn profits by lending money to borrowers. The borrowers have to pay a price for the loan; that price is called *interest*.

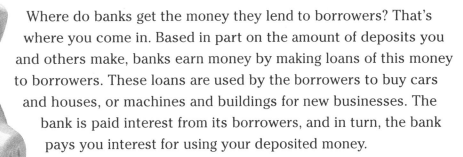

Where do banks get the money they lend to borrowers? That's where you come in. Based in part on the amount of deposits you and others make, banks earn money by making loans of this money to borrowers. These loans are used by the borrowers to buy cars and houses, or machines and buildings for new businesses. The bank is paid interest from its borrowers, and in turn, the bank pays you interest for using your deposited money.

In order to make a profit, the bank charges more interest to borrowers than it pays to savers. For example, borrowers might pay 8% interest, and savers might earn 5% interest. The difference is the bank's *markup*. The bank uses its markup to pay its employees, buy computers, and pay other expenses of the firm. The bank's return for taking a risk—its profit—is also part of the markup. Banking, like other enterprises, can be a risky business; after all, customers might default on a loan, which means the customer does not repay the loan. An understanding of banks and interest is important; it can help you make wise saving and investing decisions now and in the future.

FITNESS VOCABULARY

Interest – The price paid for using someone else's money.

Interest rate – The price paid for using someone else's money, expressed as a percentage.

Principal – Amount deposited in savings without including interest earned.

Simple interest – Interest earned on the principal and paid out to a depositor.

Compound interest – Interest computed on the sum of the principal and previously earned interest.

Compounding – The practice of leaving interest earned "on deposit" so that it too earns interest.

Rule of 72 – A formula that can be used to calculate how long it takes for invested money to double.

MUSCLE DEVELOPERS

Learn these ideas, practice them, and develop your financial fitness muscles.

✔ Banks and other financial institutions bring savers and borrowers together.

✔ Savers provide money for borrowers, and some of the interest that borrowers pay is used to pay interest to savers.

✔ Banks and other financial institutions earn profits by charging higher interest to borrowers than they pay to savers.

✔ Interest can be simple or compound.

✔ Money grows more rapidly if interest is compounded.

✔ Understanding the effects of compound interest can help people make wise decisions about saving.

Showing Your Strength

If you know the answers to these questions, you are developing some financial muscle.

1 **Why do banks and other financial institutions charge higher interest rates to borrowers than they pay to savers?** *(Banks are businesses that have expenses and want to make a profit. The difference between the interest earned by loaning money to borrowers, and interest paid to depositors, pays the expenses and provides profit.)*

2 **What is the difference between simple and compound interest?** *(Simple interest is paid to a depositor when it is earned. Compound interest is left on deposit with the principal so that it too earns interest. With compound interest, the saver is earning interest on the principal plus interest on the interest.)*

3 **What factors, other than compounding, affect the extent to which money grows in a savings account?** *(Three factors are involved: the amount of money saved, the interest rate, and the length of time savings are left on deposit.)*

4 **What is the Rule of 72?** *(The Rule of 72 is a formula that can be used to calculate how long it takes for invested money to double. Divide 72 by the interest rate to find out how many years it will take for your money to double.)*

Simple Interest

The Simple Interest Group will use this form. Your teacher will demonstrate how to complete the form.

A Deposit Cycle	B Beginning Balance (G) from previous line	C Deposited Amount	D New Balance (B) + (C)	E Rate of Interest	F Interest earned and paid out (D) × (E)	G Ending Balance (Same as D)
1	0	10	10	20%	2	10
2		10		20%		
3		10		20%		
4		10		20%		
5		10		20%		
6		10		20%		
Total						

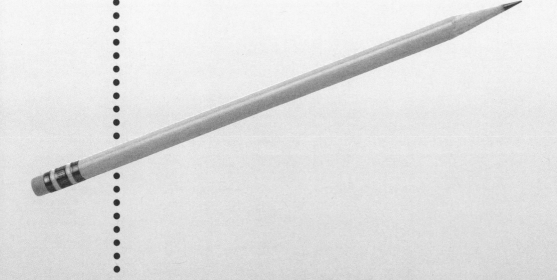

75

Compound Interest

The Compound Interest Group will use this form. Your teacher will demonstrate how to complete the form.

Round decimals to the next highest whole number.

A	B	C	D	E	F	G
Deposit Cycle	Beginning Balance (G) from previous line	Deposited Amount	New Balance (B) + (C)	Rate of Interest	Interest earned and left in acct. (D) x (E)	Ending Balance (D) + (F)
1	0	10	10	20%	2	12
2		10		20%		
3		10		20%		
4		10		20%		
5		10		20%		
6		10		20%		
Total						

Financial Fitness for Life: Shaping Up Your Financial Future Student Workouts, ©National Council on Economic Education

EXERCISE 8.2

Simple Interest: When and Why Would People Choose It?

Ms. Wirtz is a magazine editor who retired at the age of 55. She has $60,000 in an account that earns 6 percent interest annually. Because she needs the interest for some of her living expenses, Ms. Wirtz has arranged to receive an interest check from the bank every quarter (four times a year). In this way, she has money to live on, and her $60,000 principal doesn't decrease. What is the amount Ms. Wirtz receives every quarter?

The formula below shows how to calculate her simple interest and quarterly interest payments.

Principal X **Annual Interest Rate** X **Time** = **Simple Interest** ÷ **4** = **Quarterly Payment**

Ms. Wirtz' annual interest and quarterly payment are shown in the first line of the grid on this page. Use the formula to help you calculate simple interest, interest rate, principal, and quarterly payments in the rest of the grid and fill in the blank spaces.

Principal	x	Interest Rate	x	Time	=	Simple Interest	÷4=	Quarterly Payment
$60,000	x	6%	x	1 Year	=	$3,600	÷4=	$900
$20,000	x	5%	x	1 Year	=		÷4=	
	x	10%	x	1 Year	=	$1,000	÷4=	
$80,000	x		x	1 Year	=	$5,600	÷4=	
$75,000	x	9%	x	1 Year	=		÷4=	
$125,000	x	8%	x	1 Year	=		÷4=	
$200,000	x		x	1 Year	=	$14,000	÷4=	
$40,000	x		x	1 Year	=		÷4=	$500
	x	4%	x	1 Year	=		÷4=	$1,000
$100,000	x		x	1 Year	=		÷4=	$2,500

NOTE: People who hold certain kinds of interest-earning accounts, such as certificates of deposit, can have payments sent to them quarterly. That way they can use their interest for daily living expenses, travel, or other purchases. Even though they spend the interest, they maintain the principal.

Financial Fitness for Life: Shaping Up Your Financial Future Student Workouts, ©National Council on Economic Education

Racing Toward a Goal

Eight members of the Slug Hill Stock Car Team have challenged each other to begin a saving plan. They know that by making annual deposits and not withdrawing any money, their interest will compound and they will reach their goals. They also know that three things affect how their savings will grow:

▲ How much they deposit
▲ What the interest rate is
▲ How long the money remains on deposit

Even though they will all reach their goals, they will not do so at the same time. Select one of the drivers and figure out how long it will take the driver to reach the goal. Compare your results with those of other team (class) members to determine the order in which the drivers reach the finish line. Use the following charts to calculate how long it will take your driver to reach his/her goal.

Enter your results in the list below:

1st Place _____

2nd Place _____

3rd Place _____

4th Place _____

5th Place _____

6th Place _____

7th Place _____

8th Place _____

Calculate how long it will take your driver to reach the finish line and reach his or her goal.

Fill in the box at the bottom of this page.

DRIVER A
Annual Deposit = $2,000
Rate of Return = 6%
Goal = $40,000

DRIVER B
Annual Deposit = $2,000
Rate of Return = 10%
Goal = $29,000

DRIVER C
Annual Deposit = $3,000
Rate of Return = 6%
Goal = $41,000

DRIVER D
Annual Deposit = $3,000
Rate of Return = 10%
Goal = $61,000

DRIVER E
Annual Deposit = $4,000
Rate of Return = 6%
Goal = $35,000

DRIVER F
Annual Deposit = $4,000
Rate of Return = 10%
Goal = $26,000

DRIVER G
Annual Deposit = $5,000
Rate of Return = 6%
Goal = $52,000

DRIVER H
Annual Deposit = $5,000
Rate of Return = 10%
Goal = $42,000

Driver _____ wants to save $ _____
(insert letter)

It will take _____ years
to achieve the goal.

Financial Fitness for Life: Shaping Up Your Financial Future Student Workouts, ©National Council on Economic Education

Calculation Sheet for Racing Toward a Goal

A	B	C	D	E	F	G
Year	Beginning Balance (column G of previous year)	Annual Deposit (from Card)	New Balance (B + C)	Interest Rate (from card)	Interest Earned (D X E)	Ending Balance (D + F)
1	$0.00					
2						
3						
4						
5						
6						
7						
8						
9						
10						
11						
12						
13						
14						

EXERCISE

8.4 Checking Out the Rule of 72: Does It Work?

The Rule of 72 is a way of calculating how long it takes for money to double. Test how accurate the Rule of 72 is by completing the following exercise.

The formula for the Rule of 72 is to divide 72 by the interest rate. This gives you the number of years it takes to double an investment earning that interest rate.

Begin with $100,0000. With a partner and an on-line calculator, figure out when money doubles at these interest rates: 2%, 3%, 4%, 6%, 8%, 9% and 12%.

Use this website, or a similar one:

http://www.1728.com/compint.htm

Then follow these procedures:

Solve for YEARS

Input *principal:*   100,000
Input *total:*   200,000 (double the principal)
Input *rate:*   (do NOT use decimals)
Click on CALCULATE

You will get an answer in years.

Does the number of years multiplied by the interest rate equal about 72?
Complete this form using the calculator on the web site.

A	B	C	D	E
Principal	Double the Principal	Interest Rate Percentage	No. of Years for money to double (from Web Calculator)	Does Column C x Column D = approximately 72?
$100,000	$200,000	2		
$100,000	$200,000	3		
$100,000	$200,000	4		
$100,000	$200,000	6		
$100,000	$200,000	8		
$100,000	$200,000	9		
$100,000	$200,000	12		

Financial Fitness for Life: Shaping Up Your Financial Future Student Workouts, ©National Council on Economic Education

ASSESSMENT

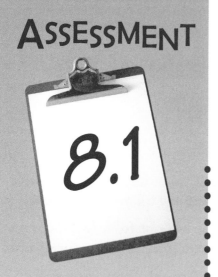

8.1

Factors That Affect How Money Grows

Three factors affect how money grows in an account:

▲ Amount of deposit
▲ Interest rate
▲ Length of time the money remains on deposit

Demonstrate these three factors by completing the grid. When you finish, make a generalization about the three factors that affect how money grows.

Beginning values:
Amount $5,000
Interest rate 5%
Time .... 5 years

Change only the amount:
Amount $10,000
Interest rate 5%
Time .... 5 years

Change only the interest rate:
Amount $5,000
Interest rate 10%
Time .... 5 years

Change only the time:
Amount $5,000
Interest rate 5%
Time .... 10 years

Year	Year Start Balance	Interest Rate	Interest Earned	Year End Balance
1	$5,000	5%		
2		5%		
3		5%		
4		5%		
5		5%		
1	$10,000	5%		
2		5%		
3		5%		
4		5%		
5		5%		
1	$5,000	10%		
2		10%		
3		10%		
4		10%		
5		5%		
1	$5,000	5%		
2		5%		
3		5%		
4		5%		
5		5%		
6		5%		
7		5%		
8		5%		
9		5%		
10		5%		

Financial Fitness for Life: Shaping Up Your Financial Future Student Workouts, ©National Council on Economic Education

LESSON 9
Stocks and Mutual Funds

Warm-Up

One characteristic of a market economy is private ownership of property. Property is not just land and real estate; it is anything of economic value that belongs to you. Your stereo is your property, a baseball card collection is your property, and shares of stock in a corporation are property, too. If you own shares of stock, you have equity in the corporation. Equity means ownership.

By owning stock in a corporation, you become part owner of that company. You can earn dividends, which are profits of the company. You can also earn a capital gain when you buy shares of stock at a low price and sell at a higher price. Your shares of stock are called *equities*.

The shares that you and other people own are generally not purchased directly from the corporation issuing them. The corporation sells a large amount of its shares to an investment banking firm in what is called an *initial public offering (IPO)*. This exchange takes place in the *primary market*. The investment firm then sells those shares to its best customers ("friends and family") in the *secondary market*.

FITNESS VOCABULARY

Capital gain – Gain from selling stocks or other investments for more than what was paid for them.

Capital loss – Loss from selling stocks or other investments for less than what was paid for them.

Dividend – Periodic payment of profit of a corporation to its stockholders or owners.

Equity – The value of property that is owned, including shares of stocks in a corporation.

Stock – A share of ownership in a company.

Primary market – Investment banks buy shares of stock directly from corporations that issue them. The stocks, in turn, are sold by the investment bankers to others.

Secondary market – Markets where stocks are bought and sold after being issued.

Stock market – Where shares of stocks are bought or sold (can be a specific, physical place or on the Internet).

Corporate bond – A loan by an investor to the corporation; the means used by corporations to raise needed money.

HOW AN IPO WORKS

Notice that the corporation issuing stock receives money for its *initial public offering (IPO)* from the investment bankers firm. This is the *Primary Market. The sale of this stock to its best customers takes place in the secondary market*

Stock exchanges provide a service. The service is to bring together people who want to buy or sell stocks. Stock exchanges "make a market" in specific stocks, just as a grocery market sells only certain brands of a good. This is also part of the secondary market.

There is no guarantee that your investment will be successful. As an owner of stocks, you have some say about how the corporation should be run. You also get to share in the profits that are made. But there is no guarantee that the corporation in which you are an owner will be successful. If the corporation does not make a profit, there is no built-in safety net or insurance to reimburse you for your losses.

Then why do so many people—now more than 50% of Americans—invest in the stock market? Many people choose to invest more of their money in the stock market rather than putting it into CDs, money market deposit accounts, statement savings accounts or U.S. Savings Bonds. People invest in the stock market because of the possibility of earning a better return.

MOST STOCK TRADES IN THE SECONDARY MARKET AFTER AN IPO

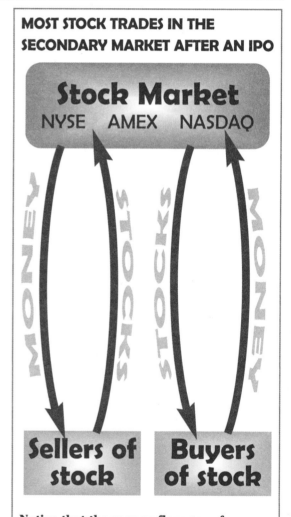

Notice that the money flow goes from the buyer to the seller of the stock, not to the business that offered the stock in the primary market.

To reduce the risk of loss, many investors follow a plan to *diversify* their holdings. Investors put their saving dollars into different kinds of investments so that possible losses in one kind are balanced by gains in another. For example, an investor might hold a combination of technology, health care and service industry stocks. They might also choose "blue chip" stocks as well as unproven, new, growth industry stocks. *Mutual funds* are based on the idea of diversification. A mutual fund company uses investor money to buy a variety of stocks. Small investors can thus invest in a greater number and kinds of stock than if they were to buy individually. The investor gains or loses based on the total fund's performance—the gains and losses of the individual stocks in the fund.

Someday, you will probably invest some of your income in the stock market. Maybe, you already do. When you invest in stock, you will be part owner of a corporation. The equity, or ownership, in the company will grow if the firm is successful. Your investment will increase in value as you share in the profits of the firm.

MUSCLE DEVELOPERS

Learn these ideas, practice them, and develop your financial fitness muscles.

✔ Stocks are riskier investments than bonds or other saving plans, such as certificate of deposits and savings accounts.

✔ Higher risk investments are not guaranteed but might produce big profits if the corporation does well.

✔ Stocks of corporations with a long history of success and a strong potential for continued growth are called "blue chip" stocks.

✔ A stock exchange makes it easy to buy and sell stock by bringing buyers and sellers together (either by phone or via the Internet).

✔ A corporation 'goes public' when it sells shares of its own stock in the primary market. The corporation raises money through this offering.

✔ After the initial public offering (IPO) of stock in the primary market, those same stocks are bought and sold by investors in the secondary market. The corporation gets no money from sales in the secondary market.

✔ Investors in stock earn a return on their investment through dividends (distribution of profits) as well as capital gains (selling stocks for more than the purchase price).

✔ Diversification is a big word that means that a lot of different kinds of investments or stocks are held. Investors diversify to reduce their risk of loss.

✔ One reason that investors buy mutual funds is to gain more diversification of their portfolio.

Financial Fitness for Life: Shaping Up Your Financial Future Student Workouts, ©National Council on Economic Education

Showing Your Strength

If you know the answers to these questions, you are developing some financial muscle.

1 **What are equities?** *(Most people refer to shares of stocks as equities, but people can also own equity through real estate or through owning their own business.)*

2 **What is meant by "buy low; sell high"?** *(When people buy stock, they hope to make a profit. In order to do this, they have to sell the stock at a higher price than the price at which they bought it. For example, if you buy 10 shares of ABC Corporation at $100 a share, and you sell it at $200 a share, you'll make a profit of a little less than a $1,000 after the deduction of a commission or fee.)*

3 **When investors buy shares of XYZ stock, do they buy it from the XYZ Corporation?** *(No. When XYZ Corporation decides to sell shares of its stock to the public, it sells those shares in the primary market — only to investment bankers.)*

4 **What is the secondary market?** *(It is where stocks are bought and sold by the public after being issued. The New York Stock Exchange, the American Stock Exchange and the NASDAQ are secondary markets.)*

5 **Why is investing in companies important?** *(When people invest in shares of a corporation, they are demonstrating their confidence in the corporation's future success. When corporations are successful, they are able to generate profits, expand operations, hire more workers, pay more taxes, disburse more dividends to the corporation's shareholders and improve the standard of living.)*

6 **What are some differences between stocks and bonds and other savings instruments offered by financial institutions?** *(Stocks show ownership; bonds and savings plans show debt. Dividends are paid to owners; interest is paid to bondholders and to those with savings plans.)*

7 **How do stockholders earn a return on their investment?** *(Through dividends and through capital gains, which is the difference between the sale and purchase price of the stocks.)*

8 **How can stockholders cut down on their risk in their stock investment?** *(Buy blue-chip stocks that carry less risk; diversify one's portfolio to include various stocks and a combination of equities and debt instruments; buy mutual funds.)*

An Interview with Mr. Stock

Role-play this interview with Mr. Stock. After hearing the interview, answer the questions that follow.

Interviewer: Hey, where are you going, Mr. Stock?

Mr. Stock: I'm on my way to a new owner. I've just been sold.

Interviewer: What do you mean—you've just been sold?

Mr. Stock: Well, you see I indicate ownership in a *corporation*—not a sole proprietorship or a partnership. A corporation is a legal entity—like a person—permitted by government. Each corporation issues stocks initially to raise money in order to pay for the things the corporation needs to make a profit—like equipment, buildings, and money to start the business. Each investor who owns one or more shares in a business is one of the owners. Some large companies have millions of owners because they have a lot of stocks and there are many investors that own those stocks.

Interviewer: Where are you bought and sold?

Mr. Stock: It depends. When I was initially issued, my corporation sold me to an investment brokerage firm. This is a place that specializes in issuing new stock. The investment brokerage paid money to my firm for me. Then the investment brokerage firm sold me to investors. I have been sold many times since I was born—mainly through the New York Stock Exchange. I am a stock of a major corporation listed on that exchange so I can be bought and sold in that place on Wall Street in New York City. Every stock cannot be traded there—only those that are listed on the exchange.

Interviewer: When you were sold on the New York Stock Exchange, your corporation must have made a lot more money.

Financial Fitness for Life: Shaping Up Your Financial Future Student Workouts, ©National Council on Economic Education

Mr. Stock: Oh no, that money went to the investors who owned the stock and wanted to sell it. The money from the sale of stock goes to the firm only when it is initially sold. After that, the sales of stock involve transferring money from the buyer of the stock to the seller.

Interviewer: You mentioned that only stocks listed on the stock exchange may be traded. Does that mean that owners of stocks not listed on that exchange have no place where they can sell their stocks?

Mr. Stock: No. There are other exchanges, such as the American Stock Exchange, where stocks are bought and sold. There are also computer exchanges where the buy-and-sell orders for stocks are processed electronically. And with some stocks, there are several places where the stocks of any company are traded.

One of these is the NASDAQ market. Now, this gets confusing, so listen carefully. The NASDAQ market is really one or more brokerage houses who *make a market* in a particular stock. Making a market means that the brokerage house is the contact point for buyers and sellers who want to trade a particular stock. Each of these brokerage houses, which makes a market in a particular stock, indicates to a centralized location through its computers, the price and number of shares traded so that other people know what is going on. So the NASDAQ is not just one stock exchange like the New York or American, but lots of places all over—all keeping those computer lines humming.

And then with very small corporations, owners sell their shares to others by advertising in some way that they are for sale.

Interviewer: That sounds very complicated. Why do individuals buy you and other stocks?

Mr. Stock: The process is really quite easy. Besides, investors think I can be *very* handsome, not in the way that you might think. Many people want to become handsomely rich through buying stocks. When people buy stocks, they become owners and can share in the profits. If the firm is very profitable, it can make the owners rich. But keep in mind that there is a downside to buying stocks— there is considerable risk. If the business does not do well, the stockholders may not get any profit. They may also lose all of their investment if the corporation goes under.

Interviewer: Isn't that a bit iffy and scary?

Mr. Stock: Sure is. But many individuals are willing to do it because they have a greater opportunity to earn higher returns than they could with some other kinds of investments, such as savings accounts, certificates of deposits, money market deposit accounts and even U.S. Savings Bonds. It's a matter of how much risk you want to take.

Financial Fitness for Life: Shaping Up Your Financial Future Student Workouts, ©National Council on Economic Education

Interviewer: So what's the difference between you and those other types of investments that you mentioned?

Mr. Stock: Stock is equity or ownership in a corporation. Bonds and savings plans are debt, not ownership. With debt, there is generally more security with your investment. The investor or saver is promised interest at certain times and a return of the loan. If the promises are not kept, the investor or saver can take legal action against the debtor to get the money. Remember, people who own me are not promised an annual return or that their investment will be returned.

Interviewer: Have any of your stock friends died?

Mr. Stock: Oh, yes. When a corporation folds, stocks die too. This could happen if they are taken over by another company or if they go out of business.

Interviewer: What is the average life of a stock?

Mr. Stock: Hard to say. Some of us live on for a very long period of time…many 'people' lifetimes. If an owner of stock dies, the stock does not die and it can be sold to someone else or inherited because the corporation still exists. Well, I must be going to my new owner. I hope I can get some rest with this new owner. This moving around is very tiring.

Interviewer: Before you go, I would like to ask one more question. Why don't your owners keep you a long time?

Mr. Stock: Some of them do. They keep me for years. I get to know them pretty well. Others get rid of me because they think they can get a better return on their money with some other type of investment. They sell me and buy something else. Others need the money to buy something like a car, house, etc. They particularly like to sell me when they have made some money on me.

Interviewer: How do stockholders make money on their stocks?

Mr. Stock: One important way is to sell the stock for more than they paid for it. Another way is when they receive dividends, which may be paid by the corporation. Dividends are the sharing of profit. Some corporations share some of their profit; others put the profits back into the business—the stocks generally increase in value because of that.

Oh, I must go before my owner gets annoyed. If you have any other questions about stock, ask your teacher.

Financial Fitness for Life: Shaping Up Your Financial Future Student Workouts, ©National Council on Economic Education

Questions to Answer

a. What is a stock?

b. When do firms receive money from a stock?

c. Where are stocks traded?

d. What are the advantages and disadvantages of owning stocks?

e. How do stockholders gain a return?

f. What is the difference between owning stocks and owning bonds or savings accounts?

g. Why are stocks generally riskier than bonds?

h. Considering that there is generally more risk in stocks than bonds or savings instruments, why do investors still put money into stocks?

EXERCISE 9.2

Juanita's Decisions

Read the following case problem and answer the questions that follow.

Juanita was very impressed with the design of the clothes manufactured by the Trendy Design Company. At the beginning of the year, she bought $3,000 worth of stock in the firm as well as a $10,000 bond of the same corporation that paid an 8 percent interest.

During the year, she was paid $200 in interest on the bond, which is about 83 percent of the amount she should have received. She did not receive any dividends on her stock investment in the firm. She was surprised to learn at the end of the year that the firm was having so much difficulty making money that they needed to liquidate the business. This means the corporation must sell their possessions in order to pay back its creditors and owners.

After the liquidation, Juanita received $2,500 for her bonds, which was her share of the proceeds. She received nothing for her stocks and no dividends.

Please answer the following questions:

1 As shown through this case, who gets paid first—owners or creditors—when the firm is liquidated? _____

2 Which investment was more risky for Juanita?

_____

3 Do you think that all stocks are riskier than all bonds? Why or why not?

_____

_____

_____

LESSON 10
Let Lenders and Borrowers Be

Warm-Up

Buying a gallon of milk is a pretty straightforward exchange. You walk into a store, grab a plastic jug, pay the cashier, and you're on your way. Saving, borrowing—and even investing—are a bit like buying products at a grocery store.

A bank, credit union, or other financial institution can be thought of as a super-market. It brings a number of products together in one place so that buyers don't have to shop all over town for what they want. At a bank, consumers can cash a check, deposit money, apply for a loan, purchase a Certificate of Deposit, or get investment advice. Many goods and services are provided by banks and other financial institutions.

One of the most important roles of a financial institution is to act as an interme-diary. Intermediaries bring together those who are in need of funds and those who wish to invest. For example, when a new company is just getting off the ground, it needs funding—for materials, equipment and supplies, maybe even to hire more workers.

FITNESS VOCABULARY

Financial intermediary – Banks, credit unions, pension funds, insurance companies, mutual funds and other other financial institutions acting to bring together savers and borrowers as well as buyers and sellers of stock.

Institutional investors – A type of financial intermediary, such as a pension fund or mutual fund, who buys stocks and other investments for clients with the goal of making money.

Opportunity cost – The next-best alternative that is given up when a choice is made.

Mutual Fund – A group that pools investor money to purchase a variety of stocks.

Somewhere out there are investors looking for an opportunity. Often it is through a financial institution that the start-up company and the investor are brought together. The company finds its funder, and the investor finds an opportunity.

In this lesson, you will learn how banks, credit unions, mutual funds and other financial institutions act as intermediaries, bringing together savers, borrowers, and investors. This information will give you food for thought as you begin to make investment decisions on your own.

92

Learn these ideas, practice them, and develop your financial fitness muscles.

MUSCLE DEVELOPERS

✔ Banks, credit unions, stock exchanges, and other financial institutions act as intermediaries, bringing together savers and borrowers, as well as buyers and sellers of equities.

✔ Investors help businesses grow. Financial institutions help investors find the right investment opportunities.

✔ Interest rates paid on loans and deposits are established by supply and demand.

✔ Financial intermediaries can provide a number of investment options.

✔ People save their money in low or non-risk investments for several reasons: they don't know enough about other forms of investing; they prefer the liquidity of a savings account; they don't want to pay the cost of a broker; they may not have enough available income to purchase the minimum denomination of stocks or bonds.

✔ Mutual funds bring together money from investors that the mutual fund company then invests in a diversified portfolio.

✔ Insurance companies and pension funds are financial intermediaries: they collect premiums and invest them in diversified portfolios.

Showing Your Strength

If you know the answers to these questions, you are developing some financial muscle.

1 **How do banks, credit unions, mutual funds, and other financial institutions act as intermediaries?** *(They provide different types of accounts for savers and investors. They attract borrowers, savers, buyers, and sellers and thus these institutions bring together those who have funds and those who want them.)*

2 **Why is a stock mutual fund considered a financial intermediary?** *(Mutual funds provide a means by which investors can own portions of the stock of many different companies. The fund brings together investors and investment opportunities.)*

3 **Why are intermediaries important to the economy?** *(Without intermediaries, investors would find it difficult to locate opportunities for investment. And without intermediaries, those in need of funds might be unable to access them.)*

93

EXERCISE 10.1

Calamity in Cow Town

Read the story below and answer the questions that follow.

Every town has at least one grocery store. In Cow Town, there are three large supermarkets. For the most part, all three markets get their groceries from the same food brokers and pay similar prices for the items they sell. This includes the milk that each market sells.

In the summer of 1982, Mrs. Jones created a new drink to serve her bridge club. She mixed milk, bananas, and pineapple juice together and called it banana milk. The ladies in the club couldn't get enough of the banana milk, and the eight ladies went through five gallons of milk, six pounds of bananas, and two gallons of pineapple juice that day. They each asked for the recipe and, on the way home from Mrs. Jones's house, they each bought two gallons of milk, along with the other ingredients.

The next day each lady made up a batch of banana milk and served it to her children, grandchildren, the neighbors, and anyone else who happened by. Everyone loved the stuff and headed for the grocery stores to get milk. Day after day, more people came to know and love banana milk, and, day after day, people bought more milk than they ever had bought before.

The grocers in Cow Town would place the usual amount of milk on the shelves in the morning, and it would be gone by midafternoon. Then it was gone by noon. Then it was gone by midmorning. Finally, the grocers were simply handing the milk to the awaiting hordes early in the morning. The grocers tried to get more milk, but there were only so many cows in Cow Town.

What could the grocers do to reduce the frenzy? There was only one answer. Each grocer raised the price on the milk. First, they raised their prices by ten cents a gallon. Then 20 cents. Then 30 cents. As they raised the price, they

94

sold fewer and fewer gallons until, one day, the milk was actually on the shelf the whole day before the last gallon was grabbed.

Yes, in the summer of 1982, the people of Cow Town learned a lesson in supply and demand. What happened to the people of Cow Town who cut their milk consumption because of the higher price? They drank orange juice instead.

Questions to Answer

1. **What happened with the demand for milk in the story? Why?**

_____

_____

2. **What happened with the supply of milk in the story? Why?**

_____

_____

3. **What happened to the price of milk in the story? Why?**

_____

_____

4. **What do you think happened to the prices of bananas and pineapple juice?**

_____

_____

5. **If you were one of the dairy farmers in Cow Town, and the price of milk went up, what changes might you have made on your farm?**

_____

_____

95

READING
10.1

Meet Me at the Stock Market

The stock market operates through financial intermediaries, such as the stock markets and stock brokers. Institutional investors are another type of financial intermediary. Examples of institutional investors are brokerage firms, pension funds, and mutual funds. They buy stocks and other investments for their clients, and their goal is to help their clients make money.

Institutional investment firms have workers who investigate corporations. They look at all of the company's business documents and check all the important financial information of the corporation, such as its income, expenses, and how it invests to make future growth possible. When institutional investors find a corporation that looks like it's going to be more profitable in the future, they buy stock in the corporation.

Brokerage firms buy stocks and bonds for their clients. Pension funds buy stocks, bonds, and mutual funds to hold for their clients' retirements. Mutual funds put together packages of stocks and bonds, organizing them into different funds. Clients can choose to buy shares in the different funds depending on their goals. If clients want to have a steady stream of money coming in without a lot of risk, they will want to invest in an income mutual fund. There is never a guarantee of no loss, but the mutual fund managers who design the income fund will do their very best to choose a package of stocks that is likely to steadily provide income.

Some clients may be willing to risk losing some of their money in exchange for the possibility of earning a higher return. In this case, the mutual fund managers put together a package containing stocks in new companies or companies with new products. This kind of fund is called a "growth fund." If these companies become very successful, the rewards for owning shares in this fund will be great. On the other hand, if the companies go out of business, or if there is very little demand for the new products, the price of shares in the fund will go down, and the client will either lose or have very little growth in the investment.

ASSESSMENT

10.1

Financial Terms

Match the terms with their descriptions.

1. The party who brings together those who need funds with those who have funds.

2. The next-best alternative when a decision is made.

3. The group who buys stocks, bonds, and mutual funds for the clients' retirement plans.

4. The difference between revenues and costs.

5. The costs of doing business.

6. Group such as a mutual fund.

7. The supplier of funds for loans.

8. The demander of loans.

9. The price of money.

a. saver

b. profit

c. institutional investor

d. opportunity cost

e. interest

f. pension fund

g. borrower

h. financial intermediary

i. operating costs

LESSON 11
Saving and Investing Are Risky Business

Warm-Up

Sir Edmund Hillary, when asked why he climbed Mount Everest, is said to have responded, "Because it is there." Hillary was a risktaker who enjoyed the good feeling he got from reaching an exciting, difficult goal.

Maybe you're a risktaker, too. Do you enjoy riding down steep hills on a snow board? Does the thought of skydiving or riding a bucking bronco make your pulse race? Would you invest all your savings to buy a rare stamp?

Risk is an important thing to keep in mind as you begin to think about investing your hard-earned income. How much are you willing to risk? How much can you afford to lose?

Because most investments involve risk, investors must examine carefully their own attitudes toward risk. They must also realize that there are different kinds of risk.

In this lesson, you will learn about several kinds of risk that accompany the act of investing. By recognizing your own attitude and tolerance of risk, you'll be better able to make responsible decisions about how to invest your income.

FITNESS VOCABULARY

> **Interest rate risk** – The risk that interest rates will rise while you have your income locked in to a lower interest rate investment.
>
> **Inflation risk** – The risk that the rate of inflation will exceed the interest rate you are earning on an investment.
>
> **Risk of loss** – The risk that the value of your investment will decrease.
>
> **Opportunity cost** – The next best alternative given up when a choice is made.

MUSCLE DEVELOPERS

Learn these ideas, practice them, and develop your financial fitness muscles.

✔ Investments that carry the greatest risk usually have the potential for the greatest reward (or the greatest loss).

✔ Every investment involves risks.

✔ Different investments have varying degrees of risk. The investor should determine how much risk she or he can tolerate when putting his or her savings to work in stocks, bonds, or savings instruments.

✔ If you commit your income to a long-term investment (such as a long-term CD or a 30-year bond), you must be prepared to accept the agreed-upon interest rate for as long as you hold that investment, even if other investment options offer higher rates of return.

✔ Figuring your rate of return on an investment is very important for comparing one investment with another.

✔ With a savings account, the principal is not at risk. Stocks, on the other hand, offer no guarantees. You might pay $50 a share for XYZ stock, and a month later, the share price could be $5. If you sell, you'll have less money than you had at the beginning.

Showing Your Strength

If you know the answers to these questions, you are developing some financial muscle.

1 **What risk is involved in a statement savings account?** *(Although a statement savings account is insured up to $100,000, there is risk. For example, while your savings earn 3% interest in the account, the inflation rate might be 4%, which means that your savings lose its purchasing power.)*

2 **What risk is involved in the stock market?** *(Even though blue chip stocks have traditionally returned more than 10% annually, there is no guarantee that they always will. The price of a stock can go up—or down. If the price goes down, investors can lose part of their original investment.)*

3 **Interest-rate risk primarily hurts what kind of investor?** *(Those who lock in their investment for a period and have difficulty getting their money out without substantial penalty.)*

4 **Why is knowing the rate of return important to the investor?** *(By figuring out rate of return, the investor can compare the return on various investments that he or she has).*

Financial Fitness for Life: Shaping Up Your Financial Future Student Workouts, ©National Council on Economic Education

EXERCISE 11.1

Now or Later?

One year ago you placed $975 in a savings account paying three percent interest. You were saving to buy one of the items listed below. The items changed in price over the year. Look at the current prices for the items. You will see that in some cases it was good that you waited. In other cases, you are worse off. Calculate the percentage change in price to discover just how much better or worse off you are. Give it a try!

Item	Last year's price	This year's price	% change
computer	$ 997.00	$ 897.30	
digital camcorder	$1,005.00	$ 954.75	
digital television	$1,000.00	$1,070.00	
car stereo system	$ 995.00	$1,074.60	
one year's wardrobe	$ 995.00	$1,094.50	

Amount in your savings account at the end of the year. _____
(Principal plus interest.)

1 Which items could you purchase with your savings if you were to buy them in the present year?

2 Which items would you have been able to purchase with your savings last year?

3 What item had the greatest percentage increase in price?

4 Which item had the greatest percentage decrease in price?

5 For which items did you lose buying power over the year?

Decisions, Decisions

Choosing the right savings method can be puzzling for savers. You have just discussed the risks of various savings plans. Apply your knowledge of interest-rate risk and inflation risk to determine what saving methods you would choose in the following situations. Be sure to explain why the method you choose is the best for the situation. Choose from a statement savings account, a U.S. Savings Bond, a money market deposit account, or a certificate of deposit (CD).

a You have savings of $100 that you need within two months and you think interest rates will be going down in the next few years.
Savings method _____ Why? _____
_____

b You have $1,000 in savings that you may need within three years and you believe interest rates will be rising over that time.
Savings method _____ Why? _____
_____

c You have $1,000 in savings that you may need within the next three years and you believe interest rates will be declining.
Savings method _____ Why? _____
_____

d You have $50 that you want to put away for your college costs in seven years. You believe interest rates will be increasing for most of those seven years.
Savings method _____ Why? _____
_____

e You have savings of $10,000 from which you need to make periodic withdrawals. You believe interest will be decreasing in the next few years.
Savings method _____ Why? _____
_____

Financial Fitness for Life: Shaping Up Your Financial Future Student Workouts, ©National Council on Economic Education

EXERCISE 11.3

Yield to the Investor

Calculate the rate of return on the following savings/investments.
Keep in mind that the formula is:

1   You put $1,000 into a statement savings account, and you do not add or take out anything during the year. You received $30 in interest during the year.

$$\frac{\textbf{Amount of Return}}{\textbf{Investment}} \quad \textbf{X} \quad \textbf{100} \quad \textbf{=} \quad \textbf{\% return}$$

What is the rate of return?

 %

2   You purchased 100 shares of stock for $50 per share a year ago. You received dividend payments of 50 cents per share four times during the year. The stock at the end of the year was worth $53 a share. What is the rate of return if you sold the stocks at the end of the year?

%

3   You purchased 100 shares of stock at $30, and earned 90 cents per share in dividends 4 times during the year. At the end of the year, the stock was still worth $30. What is the rate of return if you sold the stocks at the end of the year?

 %

4   You purchased 100 shares of stock at $50 a share. You received a $2 per share dividend during the year. The stock is worth $49 at the end of the year. What is the rate of return at the end of the year if you sold the stocks?

%

5   Which one of these investments yielded the best return for the year? If it is one of the stock returns that is higher than the return on the savings account (#1), explain why it *should* be higher.

_____

_____

ASSESSMENT

11.1

Weighing All the Risks

In this lesson, you have learned about three types of risks. For each of the following saving plans and investments, identify the major risk that you would have with each option. After naming the risk, give reasons for your response. The risks are:

A Inflation rate risk

B Interest rate risk

C Financial risk

1 Savings account _____
_____
_____

2 Certificate of deposit_____
_____
_____

3 U. S. savings bond _____
_____
_____

4 Stocks _____
_____
_____

Financial Fitness for Life: Shaping Up Your Financial Future Student Workouts, ©National Council on Economic Education

THEME 4

Spending and Credit Are Serious Business

Introduction

What's more fun than shopping?

Homework? Babysitting? Cleaning your room? Probably not.

But trying on the latest fashions, checking out a terrific new video game, tasting a delicious ice cream flavor at the mall: now *those* are fun things to do. In fact, the whole experience of shopping has nearly replaced baseball as the national pastime.

Shopping for a bargain presents exciting challenges. You begin by checking out commercials and advertisements to compare different brands. Then you probably go from store to store to find just what you want at the best price. But even though shopping is fun, it can also be stressful, especially if you find something you really want, but you don't have enough money to pay for it.

Financial Fitness for Life: Shaping Up Your Financial Future Student Workouts,
©National Council on Economic Education

What can you do if you're short of cash? You might be able to use credit to buy the item now, but you'll have to pay for it eventually—and you'll be paying interest too.

Yes, shopping can be a pleasant Sunday afternoon adventure or a disastrous assault on your finances. It's up to you. By being a wise and sensible shopper — one who looks for the best quality and price, and who pays bills on time — you'll have the foundation for sensible money management and a good credit record. Good credit combined with rational spending habits can set you on the road to your *Financial Fitness for Life*.

LESSON 12
Cash or Credit?

Warm-Up

A typical Sunday edition of the Chicago Tribune **weighs nearly five pounds. Half of the paper contains news, features, and editorials; the other half — about 2½ pounds — is advertising.**

Advertising is an important component of a market economy. It attempts to increase the demand for certain goods and services by changing people's tastes and preferences. For example, an ad that shows a famous athlete drinking a new brand of sports drink might encourage more people to buy the product. When great-looking models on a billboard are wearing designer jeans, consumers may believe buying that brand of jeans will make them just as attractive as the models.

Of course, when people respond to advertising, they may end up spending money. It might be a small amount, like $17 for a new music CD, or it could be hundreds of dollars for clothes, sporting goods, a computer, or stereo equipment. There's nothing wrong with spending money; in fact, consumer spending generates positive effects in the economy, including more jobs and income for workers and more taxes to support public projects.

But sometimes spending can get out of hand. Sometimes people spend more money than they actually have. One way they do this is by using credit.

Credit, when handled wisely, allows a person to buy a product now, use and enjoy it, and pay for it later— with interest. If there were no credit, most people would have difficulty saving enough to buy a house or a new car, and many students would not be able to go to college.

107

Just like other decisions, however, the decision to use credit involves an opportunity cost. And with credit, the opportunity cost lies in the future. When you buy that birthday present for your mom on credit, she can enjoy it right away, but you'll have to pay for it eventually. And when you do, you'll have to give up spending that money for something else you might want in order to make the payment.

Buy Now, Pay Later — **With Interest**

$50.00

$60.00

($50 + $10 Interest)

FITNESS VOCABULARY

Annual Percentage Rate (APR) – The interest rate for one year.

Credit limit – The maximum amount of credit extended to you by a bank or credit card issuer.

Finance charge – The amount of interest you must pay for the credit you use.

Annual fee – The yearly charge for having a credit card.

Minimum payment – The lowest amount you must pay toward your credit balance each month.

Grace period – A period of time during which you are not charged interest on new purchases (if you have no outstanding balance).

Late fee – A penalty, in addition to interest, that is charged if payment is received after the due date.

Interest – The price of using credit.

Interest rate – The price of using credit expressed as a percentage of the amount owed.

Opportunity cost – The next-best alternative that is given up when a choice is made.

Inflation – A general increase in prices.

MUSCLE DEVELOPERS

Learn these ideas, practice them, and develop your financial fitness muscles.

✔ Most credit is issued by banks or other financial institutions.

✔ Credit allows you to postpone paying for a product while you use and enjoy it right now.

✔ When you use credit, you have to repay the amount you owe, plus interest, at a later date.

✔ The opportunity cost of using credit lies in the future. When you pay back your credit debt, you will have to give up something else you could have bought with that money.

✔ Knowing all the details of a credit agreement will help you use credit wisely.

✔ Credit is offered at different rates and with different "other" charges. It pays to shop around for the best terms that you can get.

In this lesson you'll learn about advantages and disadvantages of using credit and about how to read a credit card statement. Knowing about credit and making good decisions about how to use it will help you control your finances now and in the future.

Every Choice Involves an Opportunity Cost

If you see a terrific looking sweater on sale for $50,

you might use your credit card to buy it right now.

But next month, when the bill for $50 comes in the mail,

you'll have to give up something else

you could buy for $50 in order to pay your debt.

The thing you give up is your opportunity cost.

Showing Your Strength

If you know the answers to these questions, you are developing some financial muscle.

1 **What are some of the advantages of using credit?** *(Using credit is safer than using cash. Because your signature is on the credit card, no one but you can use it. If your credit card is lost or stolen, you are not responsible for unauthorized purchases beyond the first $50. You are not responsible even for the first $50 if the card is used after you report the loss.)*

2 **What are some disadvantages of using credit?** *(The biggest problem with using credit is using it too much. If you charge more than you can reasonably repay, you're headed for trouble.)*

3 **What is the interest rate on a typical credit card?** *(Rates vary greatly. Some introductory rates are as low as two or three percent, but don't be fooled. Those rates can jump to 15 percent or even 22 percent when the introductory period expires.)*

4 **What's so important about the grace period?** *(The grace period tells you how many "free" days you have before the credit card company starts charging interest. Charges you pay before the grace period ends (the payment due date) are interest free. Some credit cards have no grace period. That means the bank charges interest from the day you make a purchase.)*

5 **How can you find out which bank has the lowest rate?** *(Just as you shop around for the best deal on a new bike, you should shop around for credit. Check the Internet and the business pages of your local newspaper, or call the toll-free number of banks that issue credit cards.)*

6 **How old does a person have to be to get a credit card?** *(To have your own credit card, you have to be 18, but if an adult agrees to co-sign for you, you can get one when you're younger.)*

110

EXERCISE 12.1

So Many Credit Card Offers: What's the Difference?

**With your partner, examine two credit card applications.
Then complete the chart below and answer the questions that follow.**

	Credit Card A	Credit Card B
Annual fee		
Interest rate (APR)		
Grace period		
Minimum payment		
Late fee		
Other fees		

If you were to choose one of these credit cards, which one would it be? _____

_____

What are the benefits of the card you chose? _____

_____

_____

_____

What are some of the costs of the card you chose? _____

_____

_____

_____

111

Cash or Credit?
You Be The Judge

Read the four stories below and analyze each person's spending decision regarding the stereo sale advertised above.

A

Elizabeth wants to buy a new stereo, but she just started her baby-sitting job and she hasn't earned any money yet. She figures once she starts earning income she can save $90 a month in a savings account that earns three percent interest *annually*. Elizabeth learned about *inflation* in school. Inflation is a general increase in prices. She learned that the annual inflation rate is about three percent.

She decides to save her money and buy the stereo next year when she can afford to pay cash for it.

Assuming the price of the stereo increases at the rate of inflation, how much will the stereo cost a year from now?
(HINT: $1000 x .03 + $1000) _____

2 How much will Elizabeth put into her account in the year?

_____

3 Will Elizabeth be able to buy the stereo?

_____

4 Will Elizabeth have any money left over?

_____

B David would like to buy a stereo and save 20 percent during a sale. He uses his credit card to pay for it. David is counting on getting a lot of graduation money from his parents' business associates. David knows that his credit card company offers a 28-day grace period, so if he pays off the whole amount, he won't owe any interest.

Sure enough, after his big party, David counts up the checks and he has $900! When he gets his credit card bill at the end of the month, he is able to pay the balance of $800 in full.

1 How long will it take for David to pay off the $800?

_____

2 How much interest will he have to pay?

_____

C Ryan has a credit card. When he spotted a sale, he wanted to take advantage of the $200 savings and buy a stereo at the sale price.

Ryan plans to save $90 a month from his job as an office assistant in his dad's insurance business. He plans to pay the credit card company $90 every month until his bill is paid.

1 Use the chart on the next page to figure out how long it will take him to pay off his credit card debt; the first month is done for you.

Ryan's Credit Card Summary

A	B	C	D	E	F	G
No. of Months	Amount Owed (Col. G on line before)	$90 paid each month	New Balance (B – C)	Annual Interest @ 18% (D x .18)	Monthly Interest (E ÷ 12)	New Amount Owed (D + F)
Month 1	$800.00	90.00	710.00	127.80	10.65	720.65
Month 2	720.65					
Month 3						
Month 4						
Month 5						
Month 6						
Month 7						
Month 8						
Month 9						
Month 10						
Month 11						
Month 12						
Month 13						
Month 14						

2 Add all the numbers in Column C to find out how much Ryan ended up spending when he bought the stereo.

_____

114

D

Caitlin really wants a new stereo too, and the 20% off sale is very tempting, so she decides to use her credit card and buy the stereo now for $800.

Caitlin works once in a while for her neighbor—cleaning, baby-sitting or mowing the lawn—but she doesn't really earn a regular income. She probably won't be able to save much money, so she plans to pay only the minimum required every month on her credit card bill.

(NOTE: Most credit card companies require a minimum monthly payment of at least $10 or 1/50 of the unpaid balance, whichever is higher. So, if you owe $1,000, your minimum payment is 1/50 of $1,000 or $20; if you owe $100, your minimum payment is $10 because 1/50 of $100 is only $2.)

1 Look at the chart for Caitlin's Credit Record for the first 22 months and the last 17 months of her payments. The chart shows what happens when Caitlin makes only the minimum payment. Then answer the following questions.

▲ How many years will it take to pay for the stereo:

_____

▲ How much will Caitlin spend for the $800 stereo? (Total of Column C):

_____

▲ How much interest will Caitlin pay (Column F) on her purchase?:

_____

Caitlin's Credit Card Summary

A	B	C	D	E	F	G
No. of Months	Amount Owed (Col. G on line before)	Min. paymt $10 or 1/50 of B (whichever is higher)	Balance after min. is paid (B – C)	Annual Interest @ 18% (D x .18)	Monthly Interest (E ÷ 12)	New Amount Owed (D + F)
Month 1	$800.00	16.00	784.00	141.12	11.76	795.76
Month 2	795.76	15.92	779.84	140.37	11.70	791.54
Month 3	791.54	15.83	775.71	139.63	11.64	787.35
Month 4	787.35	15.75	771.60	138.89	11.57	783.17
Month 5	783.17	15.66	767.51	138.15	11.51	779.02
Month 6	779.02	15.58	763.44	137.42	11.45	774.89
Month 7	774.89	15.50	759.40	136.69	11.39	770.79
Month 8	770.79	15.42	755.37	135.97	11.33	766.70
Month 9	766.70	15.33	751.37	135.25	11.27	762.64
Month 10	762.64	15.25	747.39	134.53	11.21	758.60
Month 11	758.60	15.17	743.43	133.82	11.15	754.58
Month 12	754.58	15.09	739.48	133.11	11.09	750.58
Month 13	750.58	15.01	735.57	132.40	11.03	746.60
Month 14	746.60	14.93	731.67	131.70	10.98	742.64
Month 15	742.64	14.85	727.79	131.00	10.92	738.71
Month 16	738.71	14.77	723.93	130.31	10.86	734.79
Month 17	734.79	14.70	720.10	129.62	10.80	730.90
Month 18	730.90	14.62	716.28	128.93	10.74	727.02
Month 19	727.02	14.54	712.48	128.25	10.69	723.17
Month 20	723.17	14.46	708.71	127.57	10.63	719.34
Month 21	719.34	14.39	704.95	126.89	10.57	715.52
Month 22	715.52	14.31	701.21	126.22	10.52	711.73

A	B	C	D	E	F	G
No. of Months	Amount Owed (Col. G on line before)	Min. paymt $10 or 1/50 of B (whichever is higher)	Balance after min. is paid (B – C)	Annual Interest @ 18% (D x .18)	Monthly Interest (E ÷ 12)	New Amount Owed (D + F)
Month 163	148.49	10.00	138.49	24.93	2.08	140.56
Month 164	140.56	10.00	130.56	23.50	1.96	132.52
Month 165	132.52	10.00	122.52	22.05	1.84	124.36
Month 166	124.36	10.00	114.36	20.58	1.72	116.08
Month 167	116.08	10.00	106.08	19.09	1.59	107.67
Month 168	107.67	10.00	97.67	17.58	1.46	99.13
Month 169	99.13	10.00	89.13	16.04	1.34	90.47
Month 170	90.47	10.00	80.47	14.48	1.21	81.68
Month 171	81.68	10.00	71.68	12.90	1.08	72.75
Month 172	72.75	10.00	62.75	11.30	0.94	63.69
Month 173	63.69	10.00	53.69	9.66	0.81	54.50
Month 174	54.50	10.00	44.50	8.01	0.67	45.16
Month 175	45.16	10.00	35.16	6.33	0.53	35.69
Month 176	35.69	10.00	25.69	4.62	0.39	26.08
Month 177	26.08	10.00	16.08	2.89	0.24	16.32
Month 178	16.32	10.00	6.32	1.14	0.09	6.41
Month 179	6.41	6.41	0.00	0.00	0.00	0.00
TOTALS		2034.04			1234.05	

Total payments!

Total interest paid!

117

Understanding a Credit Card Statement

ACCOUNT SUMMARY

Account number........	1234 5678 9876
Total credit line.............	$3,000.00
Total available credit.........	$2,612.00
Cash limit..................	$1,000.00
Cash available.............	$612.00
Amount past due/over limit......	$0.00
Statement closing date..........	1/15/01
New balance...............	$387.49
Payment due date.............	2/10/01
MINIMUM PAYMENT DUE........	$13.00

ACCOUNT ACTIVITY

Previous balance.............	$345.55
Payments..................	$200.00
Other credits...............	$0.00
Purchases.................	$207.64
Cash advances..............	$0.00
Late fees..................	$29.00
FINANCE CHARGE.............	$5.30
New balance................	$387.49

TRANSACTIONS

TRANSACTION DATE	DESCRIPTION	REFERENCE NUMBER	AMOUNT
12/20/00	Super Mart Grocers	3434BR56IA787N28	$20.75
12/27/00	Zott's Gas and Go	1212SH566ER89YL7	12.00
01/04/01	Jeff's Hardware	7070MU4747SI2433EL	24.89
01/10/01	Mark Auto Service	5757WI78728RT999Z	150.00

You may avoid finance charges by paying the new balance in full by 2/10/01
Explanation of Fees: $29.00 — Late fee

If you have any questions about your account,
call 24 hours a day:
(800) 987-6543
Mail your payment in the enclosed envelope to:
Credit Card Services
3333 Fortress Lane
Box 1110
Anywhere, U.S.A. 00001-1110

118

Refer to the credit card statement in this exercise to answer these questions.

1 By what date must the minimum payment on this bill be paid?

_____

2 On what date was a grocery purchase made?

_____

3 What is the $29 fee listed under Account activity?

_____

4 Why can't a $3,500 vacation be charged to this account?

_____

5 What is the total amount of purchases made this month on this card?

_____

6 How much of the previous balance was paid off last month?

_____

7 What is the total credit line on this credit card?

_____

8 How much credit was available at the time of this statement?

_____

9 How much is the card holder's finance charge this month?

_____

10 Why does the card holder owe a finance charge?

_____

11 Based upon this person's credit limit, purchases, payments and fees, do you think s/he is handling credit wisely? Explain your answer._____

_____

_____

_____

119

ASSESSMENT

12.1

Rubric for Evaluating Panel Discussion

Prepare a panel discussion on credit which covers the topics listed in the table. Your presentation will be evaluated according to the criteria, using the point scale.

Topics to be covered in Panel Discussion	Discussed thoroughly and accurately 2 points	Briefly discussed with some inaccuracies 1 point	Not discussed 0 points
Advantages of using credit			
Disadvantages of using credit			
APR			
Grace period			
Annual fees			
Transaction fees (late fees)			
Minimum payment and total cost			
Interesting statistics about credit			
Recommendations for wise credit use			
How inflation may affect decisions about use of credit			
The opportunity cost of credit			
Totals			
Grand Total of Three Columns			

LESSON 13
Establishing Credit

Warm-Up

Remember the fable of the boy who cried wolf? The shepherd boy made up so many stories about seeing a wolf in the pasture that when he actually did see one, no one in the village believed him or answered his cries for help. If he had been honest and trustworthy in the beginning, his story would have been accepted when he was in real trouble.

This fable also says something about what is needed in order to establish a good credit history. People who borrow money and don't return it, or who are consistently late in making payments on loans, will have a bad credit record. They will not be trusted because of their past history and will have trouble getting loans or credit cards in the future. More important, being turned down for credit can have unfortunate consequences: no college financial aid perhaps, or no new car, no house, furniture, or even a stereo or computer.

This lesson will help you understand the importance of establishing a good credit history. By being a responsible borrower in small things, you can develop good habits that lead to a favorable credit record. Then, when you are older, you will avoid problems when applying for a loan for big-ticket items, such as a car or a house.

MUSCLE DEVELOPERS
Learn these ideas, practice them, and develop your financial fitness muscles.

✔ Good credit habits begin early. Repaying loans and returning borrowed items in good condition establish lifelong patterns of responsibility.

✔ A favorable credit history includes keeping a job and home address for more than a few months, paying bills promptly, and handling debt sensibly.

✔ Establishing a good credit history at an early age increases the likelihood of obtaining a loan when a person gets older.

✔ Having a savings or checking account and other assets indicates financial responsibility and makes acquiring credit easier.

✔ When a person applies for a loan, she or he must usually present collateral, property, or some other security to guarantee that the loan will be repaid.

121

Showing Your Strength

If you know the answers to these questions, you are developing some financial muscle.

1 What kinds of risks are involved in the use of credit? *(The lender's risk is that the borrower might not repay. The borrower's risk is not being able to make the payments, thus ruining his or her credit rating.)*

2 Why do some people have to pay much more interest on their loans than other people? *(People with a poor credit rating usually must pay higher interest rates than people with good credit ratings. This is because there is a higher risk that a person with a poor credit rating will not pay the loan back. Whenever there is greater risk of default, a lender will charge a higher interest rate.)*

3 How can a person improve a poor credit record? *(A credit record is a continuous report of a person's credit history. Ongoing and responsible payment of debt will have a positive impact on a person's credit record.)*

4 What are some things that can be used as collateral? *(Valuable possessions such as property, automobiles, and financial assets can be used to guarantee repayment; however, these items are appraised at their current market value, not their original purchase price.)*

5 What happens if a person fails to repay a loan that is backed by collateral? *(The item, e.g. a house or car, can be repossessed. That means that the lender seizes the property and sells it to help pay the loan. Whatever balance remains on the contract after the sale of the item is still owed by the borrower. For example: A borrower defaults on a car loan while still owing $5,000. The lender repossesses the car and sells it, but only gets $3,000 at a used car auction. The borrower still owes $2,000 to the lender.)*

FITNESS VOCABULARY

Credit rating – An evaluation of a borrower's ability to repay a loan, based on character, capacity, and collateral.

Character – A borrower's responsible handling of past debt as well as stability in a job and residence.

Capacity – A borrower's ability to repay based on income and current debt.

Capital – A borrower's financial assets and net worth.

Collateral – Property or other valuables used as security to guarantee the repayment of a loan. The lender can claim collateral if the borrower fails to repay.

EXERCISE 13.1A

Completed Loan Application and Credit Report – Applicant 1

Loan Application, Part A

Loan amount requested: __$8000__ Length of loan: __4 years__

Monthly payment: __$194.00__ Reason for loan: __Buy a new car__

Personal Information:

(A) Applicant's name: __James Paul Anderson__ Date of birth: __9-2-72__

(S) Spouse's name: __Judith Rice Anderson__ Date of birth: __9-29-73__

Marital status (please mark one):

☐ single ☑ married ☐ widowed ☐ divorced

Address: __704 Houser Street__ Social security #: __(A) 002-92-8976__

City: __Leslietown__ __(S) 202-35-7653__

State: __VA__ Zip: __24523__

Phone: __(703) 927-0909__

Dependents:	Relationship:	Age:
Sean Stuart Anderson	son	6 mos.

Education (record only your highest level of education attained):

__(A) High school diploma__ __(S) High school diploma__

Employment (list only the current jobs held by you or your spouse):

__(A): Construction laborer__ __(S): Housewife__

__Building Contractors, Inc.__

Household gross annual employment income: __$27,500__

Approximate net annual employment income: __$22,000__

Other income: __none__

Housing information:

Do you: ☐ own ☑ rent ☐ live with others?

Monthly mortgage or rent expense: __$550__

From **Personal Finance Economics, 6–8: Money in the Middle**
©National Council on Economic Education, New York, NY

Loan Application, Part B

Current Loans Outstanding (List the lender, loan type, balance owed, monthly payment, and remaining period of loan):

1) Seventh Bank   Personal loan $1,960 $187   11 mos.
2) You Buy It Now   TV/furniture $3,000 $113   32 mos.

Credit cards (List the name of the lender, type of card, current balance outstanding, typical monthly payment):

1) Seventh Bank   VIDA Card $2,500 $45

References (You must list in the designated order: your current employer, previous employer, and nearest relative not living with you):

1) Samantha Sternwell   Building Contractors, Inc   (703) 927-7623
2) Jason Briddet   Skyscrapers, Incorporated   (703) 937-8354
3) Martha S. Anderson   Leslietown, VA   (703) 927-0098

Purpose of loan: We would like to buy a new car. Our current car is not reliable and needs repair. We would like to borrow $8,000 for four years and think we could afford the monthly payment of $194.

Credit Report

James P. and Judith Anderson

FINANCIAL INFORMATION	ITEM	BALANCE/VALUE
Checking accounts(s):	Seventh Bank	$3,000
Savings accounts(s):	Seventh Bank	$2,000
Investments:	none	
Real estate:	none	

REFERENCE INFORMATION

Landlord: Always pay rent on time. Excellent tenant. Good neighbor to others in building.

Seventh Bank: New customer but timely with payments. They took out a personal loan last month, have had their credit card for six months, and have been paying the minimum on their balance each month.

You Buy It Now: Recently opened their account. Timely payments so far.

Completed Loan Application and Credit Report – Applicant 2

Loan Application, Part A

Loan amount requested: $32,000   Length of loan: ___5 years___

Monthly payment: ___$649.00___   Reason for loan: Buy a sporty new car

Personal information:

(A) Applicant's name: ___Joey Deligh___   Date of birth: 1-5-70

(S) Spouse's name: _____   Date of birth: _____

Marital status (please mark one):

☑ single   ☐ married   ☐ widowed   ☐ divorced

Address: 9191 Edgemare Drive   Social Security #: (A) 778-90-6732

City: Leslietown   (S) _____

State: VA   Zip: 24523

Phone: (703) 927-1112

Dependents:	Relationship:	Age:
none		

Education (record only your highest level of education attained):

(A) Bachelor of Science in Marketing   (S) _____

University of Leslietown

Employment (list only the current jobs held by you or your spouse):

(A): Advertising Executive   (S): _____

Billboards Galore

Household gross annual employment income: $38,000

Approximate net annual employment income: $30,000

Other income: $2,000

You Sell It – We'll Advertise It

(personal business)

Housing information:

Do you: ☑ own   ☐ rent   ☐ live with others?

Monthly mortgage or rent expense: ___$982___

Loan Application, Part B

Current loans outstanding (List the lender, loan type, balance owed, monthly payment, and remaining period of loan):

1) Sixth Bank	Personal business	$9,000	$207	57 mos.
2) Sixth Bank	Auto	$240	$246	1 mos.
3) Wildcat Lenders	Education	$19,500	$348	67 mos.

Credit cards (List the name of the lender, type of card, current balance outstanding, typical monthly payment):

1) Sixth Bank	VIDA Card	$8,500	$125
2) Sixth Bank	Charge-It-Master	$5,000	$ 75

References (You must list in the designated order: your current employer, previous employer, and nearest relative not living with you):

1) Hayward Stephens	Billboard Galore		(803) 937-9998
2) no previous employer			
3) Ronald Deligh	Winston, CA		(909) 843-1121

Purpose of loan: I would like to buy a new car. I am about to pay off my current car and don't want it anymore. If I borrow $32,000 for five years, my payment would be $649.00 per month and I could get a Corvette.

Credit Report

Joey Deligh

FINANCIAL INFORMATION

	ITEM	BALANCE/VALUE
Checking accounts(s):	Sixth Bank	$ 500
Savings accounts(s):	Sixth Bank	$1,000
Investments:	IMF Mutual Funds	$5,000
Real estate:	9191 Edgemare Drive	$10,000*

*value of home less than what is owed on its mortgage.

REFERENCE INFORMATION

Mortgage holder: Frequently late making payments. Currently, behind one monthly mortgage payment.

Sixth Bank: Has two outstanding loans and two credit cards with our bank number. Has been late with payments in the past. Currently, up to date with both loan payments. However, credit cards are at their maximum credit limit and has been paying the minimum payment on balance owed.

Wildcat Lenders: Always pays on time.

Ronald Deligh (father): Is willing to cosign on a loan.

Completed Loan Application and Credit Report – Applicant 3

Loan Application, Part A

Loan amount requested: ___$10,000___ Length of loan: ___7 years___
Monthly payment: ___$174.00___ Reason for loan: ___Buy a boat___

Personal information:
(A) Applicant's name: ___Claudette Ransdia___ Date of birth: ___12-08-53___
(S) Spouse's name: ___Landon H. Ransdia___ Date of birth: ___8-01-54___

Marital status (please mark one):
❏ single   ☑ married   ❏ widowed   ❏ divorced

Address: ___5608 Uptown Street___ Social security #: ___(A) 209-96-1746___
City: ___Leslietown___ ___(S) 207-33-7330___
State: ___VA___ Zip: ___24533___
Phone: ___(703) 937-1990___

Dependents:	Relationship:	Age:
S. Olivia Ransdia	daughter	16
John S. Ransdia	son	13
Erin E. Ransdia	daughter	12

Education (record only your highest level of education attained):
(A) Juris Doctor   (S) Master of Arts in Education
     James Madison University   University of Wyoming

Employment (list only the current jobs held by you or your spouse):
(A): Attorney   (S): Teacher
     Jones, Barnett, & Cline   Leslie County Middle School
     Attorneys at Law

Household gross annual employment income: ___$103,000___
Approximate net annual employment income: ___$ 83,000___
Other Income: ___$ 2,000___

Housing Information:
Do you: ☑ own   ❏ rent   ❏ live with others?
Monthly mortgage or rent expense: ___$1,250___

Loan Application, Part B

Current loans outstanding (List the lender, loan type, balance owed, monthly payment, and remaining period of loan):

1) Leslietown Bank	Auto	$4,300	$145	33 mos.
2) Leslietown Bank	Auto	$8,000	$247	38 mos.
3) Leslietown Bank	College	$21,000	$293	93 mos.
4) Leslietown Bank	Motor Home	$26,000	$587	57 mos.

Credit cards (List the name of the lender, type of card, current balance outstanding, typical monthly payment):

1) Leslietown Bank	VIDA Card	$ 250	in full
2) Leslietown Bank	Charge-It-Master	$ 750	in full
3) AmeriPlan Bank	Explorers	$6,750	$1,000

References (You must list in the designated order: your current employer, previous employer, and nearest relative not living with you):

1) (A) Reginald Jones	Jones, Barnett, & Cline Attorneys at Law	(703) 599-4325
(S) Janis Franken	Leslie County Schools	(703) 927-4443
2) (A) John Becker	McKenzie, Breakman and Becker, Inc.	(703) 929-2929
(S) No previous employer		
3) Mia Ransdia	Band, KY	(502) 224-2224

Purpose of loan: We would like to buy a boat. We vacation every summer at the lake and the kids like to water ski. We would like to borrow $10,000 for seven years and think we could afford the monthly payment of $174.

Credit report

Landon H. and Claudette Ransdia

FINANCIAL INFORMATION	ITEM	BALANCE/VALUE
Checking accounts(s):	Leslietown Bank	$2,500
Savings accounts(s):	Leslietown Bank	$1,000
	AmeriPlan Bank	$4,000
Investments:	AmeriPlan Fund	$22,000
	Digitec Corp. Stock	$16,000
Real estate:	5608 Uptown Street	$67,000*

*value of home more than what is owed on its mortgage.

REFERENCE INFORMATION

Mortgage Holder: Always pay mortgage on time. We have been doing business with this couple for 20 years.

Leslietown Bank: Currently, we have four loans and two credit cards with the applicants. Have never been late with a payment in 20 years. Credit cards are always paid off in full each month.

AmeriPlan Bank: Credit card balance fluctuates between $8,000 and $0 each year with the spring. Highest balances in late summer and the lowest in early spring.

EXERCISE 13.1D

Completed Loan Application and Credit Report – Applicant 4

Loan Application, Part A

Loan amount requested: $10,000   Length of loan: 5 years
Monthly payment: $203.00   Reason for loan: Purchase a motor home

Personal Information:
(A) Applicant's name: Mr. Rhett Willis   Date of birth: 11-14-55
(S) Spouse's name: _____   Date of birth: _____

Marital Status (please mark one):
☐ single   ☐ married   ☐ widowed   ☑ divorced

Address: 14 Town Street   Social Security #: (A) 402-48-3278
City: Leslietown   (S) _____
State: VA   Zip: 40533
Phone: (883) 927-3345

Dependents:	Relationship:	Age:
Mary Jo Willis	daughter*	11
Melanie Willis	daughter*	9

*Mr. Willis's daughters live with their mother who receives $450 in child support each month from their dad.

Education (record only your highest level of education attained):
(A) Associate's Degree   (S) _____
    Leslietown Community College

Employment (list only the current jobs held by you or your spouse):
(A): General Electrician   (S): _____
     Self-employed

Household gross annual employment income: $35,000
Approximate net annual employment income: $30,000
Other income: $ 50

Housing Information:
Do you: ☑ own   ☐ rent   ☐ live with others?
Monthly mortgage or rent expense: $750

Loan Application, Part B

Current loans outstanding (List the lender, loan type, balance owed, monthly payment, and remaining period of loan):

1) Leslietown Bank   Auto $9,000 $250   60 mos.

Credit cards (List the name of the lender, type of card, current balance outstanding, typical monthly payment):

1) Bank of America   VIDA Card $2,000 $75

Credit Report

Mr. Rhett Willis

FINANCIAL INFORMATION	ITEM	BALANCE/VALUE
Checking accounts(s):	Sixth Bank	$1,250
	Sixth Bank	$2,900
Savings accounts(s):	Sixth Bank	$ 500
Investments:	none	
Real estate:	none	

REFERENCE INFORMATION

Landlord: Mr. Willis has been a tenant for four years. He always pays his rent although he has been late a couple times in the last six months.

Second/Sixth Bank: Long-standing customer. Always pays his automobile loan on time. Credit cards have outstanding balances but has made payments on them in a timely fashion.

First/Seventh Bank: Always pays auto loan on a timely basis.

Clarence Mims: Mr. Willis was a faithful and dedicated employee for 15 years before he resigned six months ago to start his own business. He buys equipment and supplies from us and always pays on time.

Thomas Willis (father):   Cannot cosign on a loan. He is elderly and has a limited, fixed income.

Purpose of loan: I would like to buy a used motorhome which is priced at $10,000. I think I can pay $203.00 over 5 years for the vehicle.

EXERCISE
13.1E

Applicant Summary Sheet

LOAN APPLICANT _____

Tell what the applicant's credit application and credit report suggest about the following:

A. Character _____
_____
_____
_____
_____

B. Capacity _____
_____
_____
_____
_____

C. Collateral _____
_____
_____
_____
_____

Would you lend money to this applicant?

☐ YES   ☐ NO

Explain why or why not.

_____
_____
_____
_____

READING 13.1

Character Counts (So Do Capacity and Collateral)

CHARACTER. You may be a fine, upstanding citizen, but if you want to borrow money, you are going to have to prove it to lenders. When you are being evaluated for a loan, the lender will review your credit history as shown on your credit report. Your credit report is a detailing of the kinds of credit you are currently being granted, the kinds of credit you have been granted in the past, and how well you maintained that credit. The lender will review your credit report, watching for the following:

▲ your record of paying your credit debts on time,
▲ your history of managing other finances, such as a checking account,
▲ your employment stability, and
▲ your residential stability.

Young people seeking to borrow money often will discover one little problem with demonstrating their character. They can't get credit without a credit history, and they can't get a credit history without someone offering them credit. Okay, it's actually a big problem. However, there are ways to solve it. A person can begin to build a credit history in the following ways:

▲ Open a checking or savings account. Maintaining a checking or savings account in a responsible manner indicates stability and good money-management habits. Don't bounce a check!

▲ Establish a department store account or layaway plan. Department stores may allow you to open an account with a low credit limit. If not, they may have a plan that allows monthly payments toward the purchase of an item.

▲ Obtain a small starter loan or credit card. Consider using a savings account as collateral for a small loan at a bank. Or ask your bank officer for a "starter" credit card, which has a low credit limit or can be secured by the cash in a savings account. Borrow only what you can comfortably repay. If you obtain a credit card, pay the entire balance on time, each month!

▲ Get a co-signer for a loan. Ask a friend or family member to co-sign a loan for you. Be sure to pay the loan off as agreed. If you don't pay, your co-signer will have to.

CAPACITY. The lender will want to know if the borrower can afford to repay the loan. To make this determination, the lender will review the following:

▲ income from all sources,

▲ current debts, and

▲ net worth (the difference between everything you own and everything you owe).

COLLATERAL. Perhaps you've heard the complaint that banks only give loans to people who don't need them. In other words, some loan applicants are told they can't get a loan because they have no assets (things of value). Their response? "If I had assets, I wouldn't need a loan!" This, actually, is an exaggeration. Lenders want to be sure the borrower has something of value that could be sold to repay the loan, just in case the borrower defaults (doesn't repay). The lender will review the following:

▲ The fair market value of the collateral (a car, a house, savings).

▲ The amount of the down payment (the amount the borrower pays up front). For instance, when you buy a car or house, you are often required to make a down payment. You put up some of the money and borrow the rest. When the borrower makes a sizeable down payment, he or she is less likely to walk away from the purchase.

▲ Insurance on collateral, to repair or replace the collateral if it is damaged.

Often times the collateral for a loan is the item for which the borrower took out the loan. For instance, if you borrow to purchase a car, the lender will use the car as collateral. If you don't make your payments, the lender will take possession of the car. You must carry insurance on the car in case it is damaged. That way, if the car is damaged, your insurance will pay for the repair, and the value of the collateral (the repaired car) is maintained. Even if the car is damaged beyond repair, the insurance company will pay the value of the car, and the lender will not lose her or her loan money.

Lenders request information regarding the three "Cs,"—character, capacity, and collateral—to determine the level of risk they will be assuming by lending money to the applicant. Risk is uncertainty of repayment. The higher the risk, the higher the interest rate. Keep in mind, that if the borrower fails to repay the loan, the lender's profits will be reduced. A person with a very poor credit rating may only be able to get credit from a "loan shark"—a word used to describe a business that charges an outrageous interest rate, often as much as 700–800 percent.

Financial Fitness for Life: Shaping Up Your Financial Future Student Workouts, ©National Council on Economic Education

ASSESSMENT

13.1

Using Your Evaluation Skills

You are the loan officer for Sixth Bank in Leslietown and have a completed loan application from one of your customers. Evaluate the loan application for Rhett Willis found in Exercise 13.1D. Then complete the following:

Describe the information the application and credit report of Rhett Willis gives you about the following:

A   Character_____

_____

_____

B   Capacity_____

_____

_____

C   Collateral_____

_____

_____

Would you lend money to this individual?   ❑ Yes   ❑ No

Explain why or why not.

_____

_____

_____

_____

_____

135

LESSON 14
Comparison Shopping

Warm-Up

In May 2000, the Big Game Lottery paid out more than $300 million to two winners. After taxes, each received about $55 million. Chances are that with that much money, the winners won't be clipping store coupons or checking newspaper advertisements for the best deal on a tube of toothpaste. But even with all that money, the winners might still shop around for a good price on a sports car, a designer wardrobe, or a piece of property on the French Riviera.

The truth is, no matter how rich or poor people are, they still need to compare prices. And for average people—those who have tight budgets and count their pennies—comparison shopping is an essential skill that can pay off in big savings and more choices. Just think about it.

FITNESS VOCABULARY

Cost/benefit analysis – A way of examining the advantages and disadvantages of economic decisions.

Opportunity cost – The next-best alternative that is given up when a choice is made.

Deceptive practices – What a business person may do to fool a customer in order to sell the customer a good or service. Misleading prices, bait and switch, and false advertising are examples of deceptive practices. These practices are not legal.

Decision-making grid – a way of helping you to compare items so you can make a wise consumer decision.

Let's say there are two hot dog stands near your school, Jo's and Sam's. The hot dogs and other items at both stands are of equal quality. Jo charges $2.25 for a hot dog; Sam charges $2.75. It's only 50 cents difference; no big deal, right? **WRONG**. If you have a hot dog for lunch every day for the three years you're in middle school, you'll save $270 by buying your lunch at Jo's instead of Sam's. Simply by being a wise shopper, you'll have extra money to buy a few music CDs, a pair of athletic shoes and some new jeans, or maybe a couple of video games.

This lesson will demonstrate that wise consumers compare prices before they buy. It will show how to shop for the best deal and how to calculate whether the 14-ounce or 22-ounce box of Frosty Fire Hydrant Cereal is the best bargain. By being a careful shopper, one who evaluates prices and products, you can improve your chances of buying quality goods and services at prices that you can afford.

136

MUSCLE DEVELOPERS

Learn these ideas, practice them, and develop your financial fitness muscles.

✔ A responsible consumer compares prices and quality before making spending decisions.

✔ Labeling and other consumer information provide facts shoppers need in order to make responsible spending decisions.

✔ Comparison shopping enables you to get more value for your money.

✔ The opportunity cost of comparison shopping is time and income. These costs may be more than what you save by comparison shopping.

✔ An informed consumer is the best protection against fraud and deceit. An informed consumer knows his or her rights and responsibilities and uses them in the market.

✔ Consumer protection agencies provide information to and protection of the consumer.

Showing Your Strength

If you know the answers to these questions, you are developing some financial muscle.

1 **Why should consumers compare prices before buying goods and services?** (*Comparison shopping enables shoppers to buy goods at lower prices; with the money they save, consumers are able to purchase more goods and services. Therefore, a wise shopper has more choices than a careless one.*)

2 **What factors should a consumer consider when shopping comparatively?** (*Price is probably the first consideration when a person comparison shops. First, the consumer should examine and compare the quality of the goods and services they plan to buy. Other factors to consider include the cost of gas if you have to drive farther to buy something at a cheaper price; the cost of shipping if a less expensive item must be mailed to you; and the time and energy you spend shopping from store to store.*)

3 **How do government regulations protect consumers?** (*Laws exist that regulate the production of goods, and many products must be approved for safety. They must meet standards of durability and quality, and the manufacturer must honor all warranties. Government also provides help for the consumer who is a victim of fraudulent business practices.*)

4 **What are the consumer's responsibilities when purchasing goods and services?** (*Consumers should read labels carefully, follow instructions, and use products in a responsible way.*)

137

EXERCISE 14.1

A Wise Person Once Said...

Write your impression of the meaning of the two adages given below.

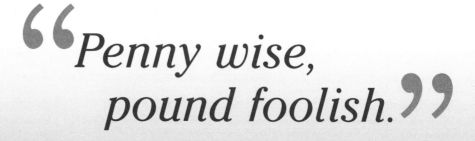

> "*Penny wise, pound foolish.*"

> "*A penny saved, is a penny earned.*"

Do the two statements agree with each other, or are they contradictory? Explain.

_____

_____

_____

_____

_____

_____

_____

_____

_____

_____

_____

_____

_____

Major Steps in a Purchase Decision

1 Identify what you want. (Our team's product assignment is...)

2 Determine how much you can spend. (Our budget for this item is...)

3 Find out what products or services are available in your price range. (Use store ads or visits, visit web sites. List these below and along the top of your grid.)

4 Choose the features you would most like to have. (List the features you definitely want and those you definitely do not want in the space below. List those that you definitely want down the left side of your grid. You might want to have a third list of "optional" features. Do not include any products containing features you do not want among your alternatives.)

5 Use the decision-making grid on the next page to analyze the alternatives.

6 Watch for hidden costs. (List any costs for necessary accessories; list any sales taxes or charges.)

7 Make your choice.

Definitely want:

Optional:

Do not want:

139

Decision-Making Grid

Features ▶ ▼Alternatives					Total Points

EXERCISE
14.3

Poor Mrs. Amos

Narrator: Mrs. Amos is an widow. She lives on a fixed retirement income. The salesman works on commission, meaning he gets a percentage of each sale he makes. The salesman is using a sales technique often reported by consumers, particularly older people. In this technique, the salesman applies pressure and tries to make the consumer feel foolish if he or she doesn't make the purchase.

Telephone rings.

Salesman: Good afternoon, Mrs. Amos. How are you this afternoon?

Mrs. Amos: I'm fine.

Salesman: That's great news, Mrs. Amos. I hope you're staying out of the heat.

Mrs. Amos: Oh, I'm trying.

Salesman: Well, Mrs. Amos. I'm with Lovely Lawns. We've been in your neighborhood lately working on many of your neighbors' lawns. We've noticed that your lawn has large, brown patches, which could indicate pest infestation or fungus. If you don't address this problem soon, you will probably lose your entire lawn.

Mrs. Amos: What should I do?

Salesman: Well, Mrs. Amos, that's the good news. We can take care of that for you. Our technician will come by your home and spray our patented pesticide and fungicide. Your lawn will be full and green again in no time.

Mrs. Amos: How much will it cost?

Salesman: Well, that's the best news yet.One application costs $48, but we will do four applications through out the summer for only $150. That's a saving to you, Mrs. Amos, of $42.

Mrs. Amos: I suppose I could have one treatment.

Financial Fitness for Life: Shaping Up Your Financial Future
Student Workouts, ©National Council on Economic Education

Salesman: I wouldn't recommend that, Mrs. Amos. We do our best to get your problem cleared up, but the treatment is only effective when it is applied four times.

Mrs. Amos: I'm afraid I can't afford more treatments than one.

Salesman: Oh, Mrs. Amos. You can't afford not to take care of this problem. After all, you don't want to be known on your block as the house with the sloppy yard.

Mrs. Amos: Well, I certainly don't want that. But I don't know how I'll be able to afford $150.

Salesman: Mrs. Amos. I completely understand. That's why we will offer you the opportunity to make installment payments for just a small fee.

Mrs. Amos: How much would the payments be?

Salesman: Well, for you, Mrs. Amos, we'll simply divide your cost into five easy payments.

Mrs. Amos: Well, I don't know. This seems like a large expense. I'm on a fixed income.

Salesman: We have many retirees as customers, Mrs. Amos. You, as well as they, can't be expected to do this kind of work yourself.

Mrs. Amos: I still don't know if I should do this.

Salesman: Mrs. Amos, if you don't mind my saying, I don't know how you can pass this up. What will your neighbors think of you if your yard becomes even worse? It's already looking pretty bad.

Mrs. Amos: Well, I guess I'll do it then.

Salesman: Mrs. Amos, you've made the right decision. We'll be out tomorrow to begin the treatments. Please hold the line so that we may make a tape-recorded verification of your purchase.

Narrator: Mrs. Amos verified the sale and began the treatment. She later began receiving her installment invoices charging one-fifth of the fee plus a 20 percent interest rate.

THE END

After reading or listening to this situation, answer the following questions.

1 What tactics did the salesman use to convince Mrs. Amos to sign up for the service?

_____

_____

_____

2 If Mrs. Amos was uncomfortable with the salesman's tactics, what should she have done?

_____

_____

_____

3 Why did Mrs. Amos stay on the phone and ultimately buy the service?

_____

_____

_____

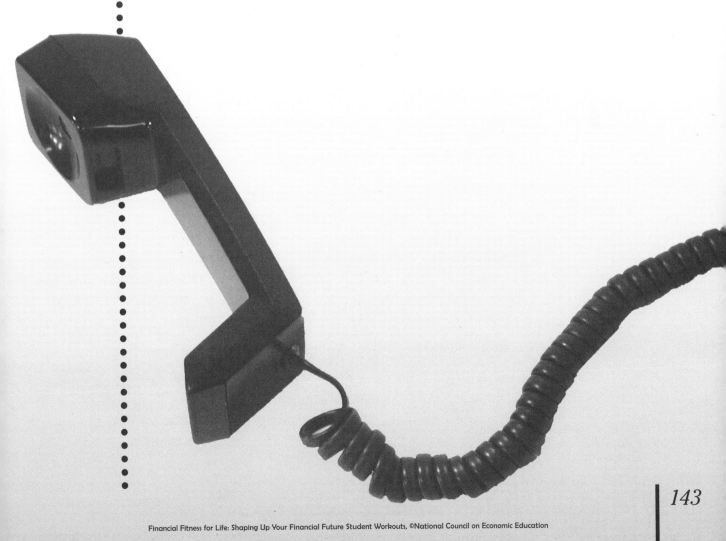

EXERCISE 14.4

The Worm Has Turned

Salesman: Hi, I'm Steve Swank. What can I do for you?

Tina Allen: I'm interested in the 1992 XYZ on your lot. What can you tell me about it?

Salesman: Oh, that's a nice one. I guess you just recently got your driver's license. Am I right?

Mr. Allen: Yes, Tina just got her license. She'll need a car to get back and forth to school. We simply have too many people and not enough cars.

Salesman: Boy, I know how that goes. I have three teenagers myself. Is this your first driver?

Mr. Allen: Yeah, Tina's our first.

Salesman: Well your little girl really knows her cars, doesn't she? She's picked the peach of the lot.

Tina Allen: *(slightly exasperated)* Could you tell us a little about the car?

Salesman: Certainly. I see in the file that it has 160,000 miles on it. Those were all highway miles, Tina. May I call you Tina? *(He doesn't wait for an answer, but continues his sales pitch.)* The previous owner never had a bit of trouble with it. It is loaded with options, too. You can see the great shape it's in.

Tina Allen: Could you tell me your asking price?

Salesman: Well, Tina, we've listed it for $5,000, but it's been on our lot for over a week now, and we like to turn our inventory over much more frequently than that. We have very strict standards for the used cars we will place on our lot, so they usually go very fast. As a matter of fact, I had a customer who was very interested in this car in here just yesterday. He said he would be stopping back later today.

Tina Allen: $5,000 is a little out of my price range. Could you do anything for us?

Salesman: Gee, I don't know, Tina. With that customer coming back in this afternoon, and all, I might be doing myself damage by coming down on the price. But, I like you. And, I have teenagers myself. I know how important it is to be seen in a hot car, am I right? *(The salesman winks at Mr. Allen.)* I'll tell you what. I'll come down to $4,800.

Tina Allen: That's still a little high. Could you bring the price down to $4,200?

Salesman: Wow, that would certainly put us at a loss. I can't see any way for us to come down that low for this fine car.

Tina Allen: Well, $4,200 is all I have budgeted for a car. I can't go any higher.

Salesman: I see your dilemma. And, I like you two. Let me go ask my manager. But, I've got to warn you. He's going to think I'm nuts for even suggesting this price.

The salesman meets with the manager in the corner of the room. The two act as though they are arguing over the price. The salesman comes back to the desk.

Salesman: Mr. Allen, Tina, I tried. He would only come down to $4,500. That's his final offer. Even at that price, we're losing money on this car. He thinks I'm crazy. I had to pull in some favors for this one. But, as I told him, you're nice people who need a car, and that's why we're in business. We figure you'll tell your friends that you got a good deal here.

Tina Allen: That's still above my budget.

Salesman: Tina, we can certainly work out a payment plan to fit your budget. Don't think of it as $4,500. Think of it as only $125 a month. You can certainly afford that, can't you Tina?

145

Tina Allen: For how many months?

Salesman: Only 60.

Tina Allen: That's a long time. The car might not even last that long.

Salesman: I don't see why not. It's been very well maintained. You know, my son's friend drives one of these, and he has 250,000 miles on it. It runs like a top. He's never had a day of trouble.

Mr. Allen: Well, I don't know.

Salesman: Mr. Allen, Tina, I can't tell you which way you should go on this. All I can say is that this is one nice vehicle, and I have a customer ready to buy it this afternoon.

Tina Allen: Well, I guess we'll have to leave it for your other customer. Thanks for your time. Good-bye.

After reading or watching this exercise, answer the following questions.

1 **In what ways did the salesman try to get Tina and Mr. Allen to see him as a friend?**

_____

_____

2 **In what ways did the salesman try to push Tina and her dad to buy the car?**

_____

_____

3 **Did you think Tina was going to buy the car?**

_____

_____

4 **Do you think Tina did the right thing?**

_____

_____

Financial Fitness for Life: Shaping Up Your Financial Future Student Workouts, ©National Council on Economic Education

READING 14.1

Comparison Shopping

About Comparison Shopping

Comparison shopping is the process of considering prices and features of similar products before making a purchase decision. The more expensive or complex an item, the more a smart shopper will want to compare a variety of options before choosing one. Comparison shopping must take into account a variety of factors such as differences in features, sizes, product quality and performance, price, and service agreements.

Advantages of Comparison Shopping

▲ You can save money, since prices for the same or similar products may vary dramatically from place to place.

▲ You may be able to get more features or value for the same amount of money.

▲ You can buy a better quality product that will last longer or perform better.

▲ You can learn about options and products you weren't aware of before.

▲ You will feel more secure that your money was spent wisely.

Disadvantages of Comparison Shopping

▲ Comparison shopping takes time, which could be used to earn money, do 'fun things,' or take care of family responsibilities.

▲ Comparison shopping may cost money, for instance, for telephone calls or gas to visit different stores.

▲ The savings from comparative shopping, especially for lower priced items, may be less than the cost of your time, gas, or other expenses.

Requirements for Comparison Shopping

▲ Access to *reliable information*.

▲ *Time* to check with a variety of vendors, and to wait for sales, special selling seasons, or inventory closeouts.

▲ The *money* to purchase an item quickly if a tremendous opportunity arises.

READING 14.2

Liar, Liar, Pants on Fire

Deceptive advertising. Producers always want to present their products in the best light. Some advertisements may contain out-and-out falsehoods, while others simply may not present the whole story. The best advice is, if it seems too good to be true, it probably is! Toothpaste advertisements may promise whiter teeth in 30 days. How, exactly, is that comparison made? How often must you use the toothpaste in order to achieve the promised results? Won't most toothpastes whiten teeth? When the packaging shows a statement that "9 out of 10 dentists recommend this Brand X," does it mean they actually recommended Brand X or does it mean they recommended the *ingredients* in Brand X (which are the exact same ingredients in a dozen other brands)?

Bait and switch. While seeking information by reading through store ads, you will often come across some mighty good bargains, usually presented on the front page. Most often these are perfectly legitimate sales designed to bring your attention to the store. However, some companies may engage in an illegal practice called "bait and switch," when the quantities of the sale item are low or maybe not available at the store at all. The salesperson will apologize for the unavailability of the sale item but direct the consumer's attention to a much nicer, more expensive, item offered at a similar discount. The seller is "baiting" the consumer by offering the terrific sale item and then "switching" the consumer's attention to another, more expensive, product. The consumer, already at the store and ready to make a purchase, will often buy the alternative item. He or she may later discover that the item purchased was available at a lower price elsewhere.

Pricing. Although a store cannot claim that the price of a product has been reduced if it hasn't been, it can use other terminology that deceives the consumer into thinking that the item is being offered at a lower price. For instance, some stores may cover the original shelf tag with a brightly colored tag stating "Special Value" or "In-store Special." The store isn't saying that this price is lower than the retail price, but the implication to the consumer is that the price for the good has been reduced. Here's a tip: pull the colorful tag aside and observe the regular price of the good. You might find that the prices are identical.

Financial Fitness for Life: Shaping Up Your Financial Future Student Workouts, ©National Council on Economic Education

ASSESSMENT

14.1

Major Steps in a Purchase Decision

5 Use the decision-making process.

1 Identify what you want.

6 Watch for hidden costs. (List any costs for necessary accessories; list any sales tax variance.)

2 Determine how much you can spend.

7 Make your choice.

3 Find out what products or services are available in your price range. (Use store ads or visits, visit web sites. List these along the left side of your grid.)

4 Choose the features you would most like to have. (List the features you definitely want, those that are optional, and those you definitely do not want in the space below. List those that you definitely want and those that are optional along the top of your grid.)

Definitely want:

Optional:

Do not want:

150

ASSESSMENT CONTINUED

Decision-Making Grid

Features ▶ ▼Alternatives					Total Points

Financial Fitness for Life: Shaping Up Your Financial Future Student Workouts, ©National Council on Economic Education

THEME

5

Get a Plan: Get a Grip on Life

(Money Management)

Introduction

Newspaper reporters are taught to answer these questions: Who? What? Where? When? How? Why? You've probably been told to think about those same questions when you study for a science or social studies test, or when you analyze a novel or short story. The **W** and **H** Questions can help you make sense of important information, and they can also apply to financial matters.

 Of course, it's you.

 Learn how to manage money

 Bank, credit union, savings and loan, stock market, Internet, newspapers, magazines.

 The sooner, the better; right now is a good time to start.

 Budgeting, saving, investing.

 To prepare for a secure financial future.

152

LESSON 15
Managing Cash

Warm-Up

Every year, many families spend hours and hours planning a vacation. They look through travel brochures and check Internet web sites. They do research at their local libraries; they ask friends, relatives, and professional travel agents for suggestions. Then they sit down with maps and itineraries, planning the routes they'll take and the sites they'll visit. They might even make reservations months in advance. They know from experience that the better their plan, the more likely they are to have an enjoyable time.

Being a good money manager requires planning too. The good news is that you don't have to be a professional to be good at it. Just as families learn from their previous vacation experiences, you can review the strengths and weaknesses of your past spending decisions. Just as travel agents draw routes and select highways to specific end points, you can map out your goals for financial success. These goals become the foundation for your budget, which is a statement of your projected income and expenses. Then, when your budget is in place, you'll be ready to save and spend responsibly. Of course, just as an unexpected detour means a change of plans on a vacation, unforeseen circumstances may cause you to adjust your budget. For example, your class trip may cost more than you expected, or you may have to get a new band uniform. That's when an emergency fund comes in handy.

In this lesson, you will learn how to design a budget. You will start by examining your expenses; then you will evaluate your income. Being able to keep your expenses lower than your income will help you meet short-term goals now. More important, sticking to a sensible budget is a skill that you will use as you work to achieve long-term goals for your future.

FITNESS VOCABULARY

Fixed expenses – Expenses that cannot be easily changed and that remain essentially the same from month to month (e.g., monthly car loan payment).

Variable expenses – Expenses that can be controlled and that change from month to month (e.g., long-distance telephone bill).

Periodic income – Income not earned on a regular schedule (e.g., occasional baby-sitting, summer jobs, gifts from relatives).

Budget – A plan for managing income and expenses.

Opportunity cost – The next-best alternative that is given up when a choice is made.

Trade-off – Giving up some of one thing in order to acquire more of another.

Financial Fitness for Life: Shaping Up Your Financial Future Student Workouts, ©National Council on Economic Education

MUSCLE DEVELOPERS

Learn these ideas, practice them, and develop your financial fitness muscles.

✔ Successful money management requires a realistic analysis of income and expenses.

✔ Saving should be considered a fixed expense. By "paying yourself first" you can develop the habit of regular saving for goods and services you want to buy in the future.

✔ Periodic adjustments of a budget will occur as income or expenses change.

✔ If income is used to pay one expense, it cannot be used for something else. The opportunity cost is the next-best alternative.

Showing Your Strength

If you know the answers to these questions, you are developing some financial muscle.

1 **What is meant by the expression 'pay yourself first?'** *(Most financial advisors suggest saving a fixed percentage [usually 10–15%] of your income. If your bank allows direct deposit of your paycheck, you can instruct the bank to put a certain amount into your savings account and the rest into your checking account every time you get paid. That way, you will develop a regular saving plan.)*

2 **Is a budget necessary if a person has only periodic income and expenses?** *(Even if you don't have a regular job, or monthly rent or car payments, a budget is still a good idea because it will help you analyze your earnings and spending habits.)*

3 **Why should a student have a budget?** *(Surveys indicate that U.S. students spend more than $20 billion a year, most of it on food, clothing, and entertainment. Creating a budget can help you achieve short-, medium-, and long-term savings goals for buying the things you want.)*

4 **What is the best way to set up a budget?** *(There is no right or wrong way to create a budget. Some people use computer programs; others estimate their income and expenses with paper and pencil. The method is not so important as having the determination to stick to the budget that you design.)*

5 **How important is record-keeping?** *(After a budget is established, it's a good idea to record all actual income and expenses. This information can help determine whether a budget is realistic, or if it has to be adjusted.)*

EXERCISE 15.1

Keeping Track of Cash Flow

Have you ever spent a day at the mall with your friends and wondered where all your money went? You may have started the day with $50 in your wallet, and by 8 p.m. you don't even have enough cash for a burger and fries at the local fast food restaurant. What happened?

Money has a way of getting spent—a little bit here, a little bit there—almost on its own. You'll probably be surprised to see how a little bit here and a little bit there can add up to a lot of spending in just a week.

Use the chart below to record every expense you have for a week. Indicate whether the expense is for Food (**F**), Clothing (**C**), Entertainment (**E**), or Other (**O**) by placing the amount you spend in that column. Also note if it was a planned (**PL**) or unplanned (**UN**) expense, and identify each expense as Fixed (**FX**) or Variable (**VR**). If you need more space, set up a separate sheet of paper in the same way.

After you have kept this record of expenses for one week, total each column with numbers. This tells you how much you spent in each category. Add those figures together for a grand total. Use the grand total to calculate the percent spent for each category. Count up how many expenses were planned and how many were planned. Do the same for the fixed and variable column. Now you are ready to answer the questions on the next page.

Date	Item/ Service	(F) Food	(C) Clothing	(E) Enter- tainment	(O) Other	(PL) or (UN)	(FX) or (VR)
Ex. 5/1	Snacks	$1.56				UN	VR
Totals							
Percent							

Grand Total (F +C + E + O) =

Use the information on your expense chart to answer these questions:

1 For which of your expenses did you plan ahead of time?

2 Which expenses were unplanned—that is, bought on the spur of the moment?

3 If you had the week to do over, which expenses would you change? Explain.

4 Which unplanned expenses were bad decisions? Explain.

5 Which unplanned expenses were good decisions? Explain.

6 Which is the easiest expense to decrease, fixed or variable?

7 Which of the expenses would be easiest for you to decrease if you needed money for an emergency purchase?

EXERCISE 15.2 Living Within Their Means

Read one of the case studies on this or the following pages and decide whether the person stayed within his or her budget. (NOTE: All incomes are <u>after</u> income taxes have been paid.) Then answer questions 1-4 at the end of the exercise. After each group gives a report, answer questions 5-9.

Case Study A

Lauren earns $43,000 a year as a teacher in a booming suburban school district. She has the following monthly expenses:

Savings	$ 200
Rent/home mortgage	650
Utilities	300
Phone/cable/Internet	150
Food/groceries	225
Car payment	550
Insurance (car/rental/home)	156
Transportation, incl. gas	77
Charity	80
Clothes	55
Loan payments	450
Entertainment	200
Services (cleaning, hair dresser)	150
Other	166

Did Lauren spend more or less than she earned? _____
How much?_____

Case Study B

Brian has a retirement pension of $35,000 a year. He has the following monthly expenses:

Savings	
Rent/home mortgage	$ 185
Utilities	725
Phone/cable/Internet	240
Food/groceries	175
Car payment	207
Insurance (car/rental /home)	365
Transportation, incl. gas	148
Charity	88
Clothes	89
Loan payments	115
Entertainment	307
Services (cleaning, hair dresser)	150
Other	125
	185

Did Brian spend more or less than he earned? _____
How much?_____

Case Study C

Maria is a pre-med student, but she works part-time as a lab assistant at the university. She earns $37,000 a year and has the following expenses.

Savings	$ 100
Rent/home mortgage	575
Utilities	285
Phone/cable/Internet	225
Food/groceries	375
Car payment	125
Insurance (car/rental/home)	220
Transportation, incl. gas	47
Charity	20
Clothes	185
Loan payments	607
Entertainment	165
Services (cleaning, hair dresser)	75
Other	150

Did Maria spend more or less than she earned? _____

How much? _____

Case Study D

Suzanne is the executive vice president of a Silicon Valley computer-engineering firm. She earns $130,000 a year and has the following expenses.

Savings	
Rent/home mortgage	$1,485
Utilities	4,005
Phone/cable/Internet	550
Food/groceries	275
Car payment	275
Insurance (car/rental/home)	750
Transportation, incl. gas	625
Charity	375
Clothes	550
Loan payments	225
Entertainment	750
Services (cleaning, hair dresser)	450
Other	365
	255

Did Suzanne spend more or less than she earned? _____
How much? _____

Case Study E

Marcus is an attorney working as a prosecutor in a small town in Iowa. He earns $67,000 a year and has the following expenses.

```
Savings ......................................$ 650
Rent/home mortgage ......................... 1,275
Utilities................................... 285
Phone/cable/Internet........................ 95
Food/groceries.............................. 275
Car payment ................................ 350
Insurance (car/rental/home) ................ 215
Transportation, incl.gas ................... 85
Charity..................................... 95
Clothes..................................... 150
Loan payments .............................. 1,385
Entertainment............................... 285
Services (cleaning, hair dresser) .......... 95
Other....................................... 275
```

Did Marcus spend more or less than he earned? _____
How much? _____

Case Study F

Jeff is a successful superintendent for a small construction company in Texas. He earns $28,950 a year and has the following monthly expenses:

```
Savings ..................................$ 200
Rent/home mortgage ....................... 750
Utilities................................. 65
Phone/cable/Internet...................... 45
Food/groceries............................ 95
Car payment .............................. 155
Insurance (car/rental/home) .............. 115
Transportation, incl. gas ................ 115
Charity................................... 55
Clothes................................... 40
Loan payments ............................ 595
Entertainment............................. 45
Services (cleaning, hair dresser) ........ 60
Other..................................... 75
```

Did Jeff spend more or less than he earned? _____
How much? _____

Financial Fitness for Life: Shaping Up Your Financial Future Student Workouts, ©National Council on Economic Education

Respond to the following questions about the person whose case study your group analyzed:

1 The person's car needs a new timing belt at a cost of $700. What changes would you make in his/her budget? _____

2 If the person increases savings by $175 for four months in order to buy the timing belt, what are some trade-offs to consider? _____

3 Remember that opportunity cost is the next-best alternative that is given up when a choice is made. Based upon the choice s/he made to increase savings for the timing belt, what is the opportunity cost? _____

4 Make some suggestions for how the person whose case study you read could budget her/his income and expenses more wisely. _____

_____

_____

_____

_____

Exchange information with other teams in your class to answer these questions:

5 Who had the most money left at the end of the month?

_____

6 Who overspent the budget?

_____

7 Which worker had between $100 and $200 left at the end of the month?

_____

8 How much income did Marcus have left over at the end of the month?

_____

9 If Lauren chooses to take a trip this month that costs $500, what are some trade-offs she'll have to consider? _____

ASSESSMENT 15.1

Tomorrow Never Budgets

Evaluate the budget of James Bond, double-agent and all-around cool guy. Use the income and expense information given, and analyze his money management skills.

Income

Annual salary (take-home, net) $1,575,654
Bonus for apprehending spies (net) 65,000
Gifts from foreign dignitaries (net) 14,000
Auto, meals, travel and clothing allowance 320,000
Total Income _____

Expenses

Savings $165,987
Restaurant meals 82,999
Air plane tickets 89,454
Auto cost and maintenance 87,500
Clothing 75,009
Concert tickets 5,367
Opera tickets 4,389
Ballet tickets. 3,567
Furniture 76,456
Oil paintings. 235,643
Yacht and maintenance. 132,654
Private plane and maintenance 354,762
Maintenance of home in France 113,231
Maintenance of home in Colorado. 97,543
Maintenance of home in Hawaii. 175,432
Charity 274,123
TOTAL EXPENSES _____

▲ Are James Bond's expenses (**<** , **=** , **>**) his income? (Circle the right answer.)

▲ If Bond decides to buy a new plane for $175,000, what is his opportunity cost? _____

▲ Bond's financial advisor said he should save 15% of his income; how much is that? _____

▲ If Bond follows the advisor's advice, what are some trade-offs he'll have to consider? _____

_____

LESSON 16
Choosing and Using a Checking Account

Warm-Up

Buying a new stereo is not a snap decision. You have to know what the system has to offer: what kind of speakers does it have? Is the CD player programmable? How many stations on the FM band can be stored in its memory?

In addition, you have to think about how you will use the stereo. Do you have lots of old cassette tapes? If so, you'll want a tape player, maybe even a double. Does your music collection include old vinyl LP's of the Beatles from your father's collection? That means you'll need a turntable, too. Is your room tiny and cramped? That means you'll probably want small components that deliver big sound. And if you share a room, you better make sure you have headphones too!

If you analyze how you'll use your stereo and check out lots of options before you buy, you'll most likely choose the one that's best for you. Deciding on the right checking account (at a bank, savings and loan, credit union, etc.) is somewhat like deciding on the right stereo. You need to know what's available and how you'll use it.

This lesson introduces you to checking accounts. You'll learn about the advantages and disadvantages of a checking account, as well as how to open and use

FITNESS VOCABULARY

ATM – Automatic teller machine.

Debit card – A plastic card that is used to deduct funds automatically and immediately from a checking account.

Deposit – Adding money to an account.

Withdrawal – Subtracting money from an account.

FDIC – Federal Deposit Insurance Corporation. Institutions that have an FDIC designation guarantee your savings up to $100,000.

Interest – Money paid for the use of someone else's money.

Service charge – The fee charged by a financial institution for certain services it provides to customers.

Overdraft – Writing a check for an amount that is more than is in an account.

PIN – Personal Identification Number; a confidential code used to access private financial information or to make a transaction.

one sensibly. By making sound decisions (either for a stereo or for where to put your hard-earned money), you'll be well on your way to a future of financial security.

MUSCLE DEVELOPERS

Learn these ideas, practice them, and develop your financial fitness muscles.

✔ When choosing a checking account, you should examine a number of alternatives, based on criteria that are important to you, such as the bank location, fees, services offered, etc.

✔ Electronic and online banking offers convenience but also involves issues of confidentiality.

✔ It is the responsibility of the consumer to keep track of all transactions involving a debit card.

✔ All financial institutions have fees and charges for various services. It is wise to find out about the costs of an account before opening one.

✔ A checking account is a real convenience, but you have to be responsible about recording all deposits and withdrawals.

✔ Never share your confidential financial information with anyone.

Showing Your Strength

If you know the answers to these questions, you are developing some financial muscle.

1 **How does an automatic teller machine (ATM) work?**
(By inserting a plastic card and your PIN [personal identification number], you can use an ATM to make deposits or withdrawals in a checking or savings account.)

2 **What is the difference between a debit card and a credit card? (***A debit card is like a plastic checking account. When you use a debit card, you are actually withdrawing money from an existing account. If you try to use your debit card for more than you have in the account, you'll get an error message, and your purchase will be denied. A credit card, on the other hand, is like a loan. When you sign a credit card receipt you are agreeing to repay the credit card company—in the future—the amount of the purchase. If you don't repay the full amount by a certain date, you will have to pay interest.)*

Financial Fitness for Life: Shaping Up Your Financial Future Student Workouts, ©National Council on Economic Education

3 **What happens if you write a check for more than you have in your checking account?** *(Your check will be returned to you and you will receive an NSF [non-sufficient funds] notice. Most savings institutions will add an NSF charge to your monthly statement as a penalty.)*

4 **What other service charges might be added to your account?** *(Some financial institutions apply fees for every check you write in certain checking accounts or charge a monthly service fee. Other fees may be charged if your balance is too low, if you use the ATM of another financial institution, or if you require the services of a teller. Fees are usually charged for other special services, such as obtaining traveler's checks or money orders.)*

5 **Is money always safe in a savings or checking account?** *(If a financial institution displays the FDIC sign [Federal Deposit Insurance Corporation], you can be sure that your money in checking or savings account is insured up to $100,000. Even in bad economic times, you're guaranteed to get all your money if you need to withdraw it—up to $100,000.)*

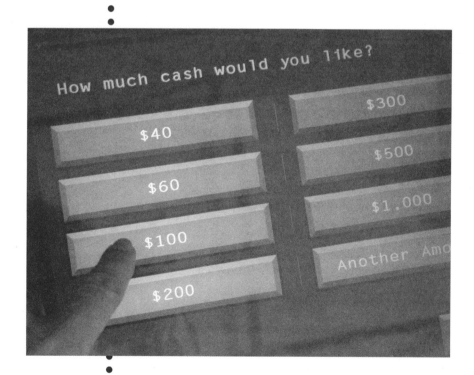

164

Design a Check

You've probably handled a check or two. Could you reproduce a check without looking at one? Use the following area to design a check. Be sure to include all of the information provided on a check.

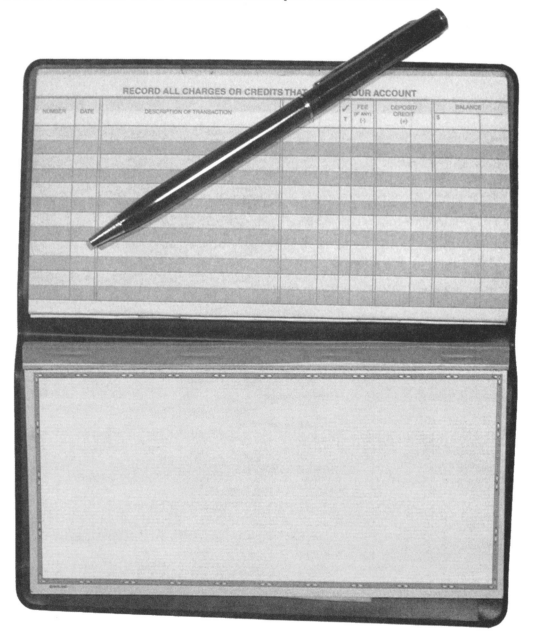

Using a Checking Account

Complete the checkbook register with the following transactions. Use Exercise 16.3 to write a check for those involving a payment by check.

Sept. 2	Beginning balance in your checking account was $145.52.
Sept. 4	Wrote check #8452 for $9.88 to Gibson's Record Shop for a new tape.
Sept. 8	Deposited paycheck for $66.95 from part-time job.
Sept. 11	Wrote check #8453 for $24.50 to Grayson's Service Station for oil change.
Sept. 15	Wrote check #8454 for $15.00 to Acme Jewelers as deposit for class ring.
Sept. 19	Stopped by ATM to withdraw $40 cash.
Sept. 22	Deposited paycheck for $63.88.
Sept. 23	Wrote check #8455 for $5.00 to pay back borrowed money.
Sept. 26	Wrote check #8456 for $13.75 to American Publishing for subscription.
Sept. 27	Wrote check #8457 for $28.63 to Neighbor's Store for mother's birthday gift.
Sept. 29	Deposited $10.00 earned for baby-sitting.
Sept. 30	Automatic withdrawal of $47.56 from checking account for monthly auto loan payment
Oct. 1	Monthly statement showed a service charge of $4.90 was debited from account.

CHECK #	DATE	TRANSACTION DESCRIPTION	WITHDRAWAL/ SUBTRACTIONS	✓ T	FEE IF ANY	DEPOSIT/ ADDITIONS	BALANCE 145 52

PLEASE BE SURE TO DEDUCT CHARGES THAT AFFECT YOUR ACCOUNT

Sample Checks

John Q. Public 123 Money Lane Richmondville, NC 27710 123-456-7890	8452

Date _____, 20_____

Pay to
the order of _____ | $ [＿＿＿＿]

_____ Dollars

Bank of America.

Sample only. Not negotiable.

MEMO _____

A011000010A 0987654321C 8454

John Q. Public
123 Money Lane
Richmondville, NC 27710
123-456-7890
8453

Date _____, 20_____

Pay to
the order of _____ | $ [＿＿＿＿]

_____ Dollars

Bank of America.

Sample only. Not negotiable.

MEMO _____

A011000010A 09876543210C 8455

John Q. Public
123 Money Lane
Richmondville, NC 27710
123-456-7890
8454

Date _____, 20_____

Pay to
the order of _____ | $ [＿＿＿＿]

_____ Dollars

Bank of America.

Sample only. Not negotiable.

MEMO _____

A011000010A 09876543210C 8456

John Q. Public
123 Money Lane
Richmondville, NC 27710
123-456-7890
8455

Date _____, 20_____

Pay to
the order of _____ | $ [＿＿＿＿]

_____ Dollars

Bank of America.

Sample only. Not negotiable.

MEMO _____

A011000010A 09876543210C 8457

John Q. Public
123 Money Lane
Richmondville, NC 27710
123-456-7890
8456

Date _____, 20_____

Pay to
the order of _____ | $ [＿＿＿＿]

_____ Dollars

Bank of America.

Sample only. Not negotiable.

MEMO _____

A011000010A 09876543210C 8458

John Q. Public
123 Money Lane
Richmondville, NC 27710
123-456-7890
8457

Date _____, 20_____

Pay to
the order of _____ | $ [＿＿＿＿]

_____ Dollars

Bank of America.

Sample only. Not negotiable.

MEMO _____

A011000010A 09876543210C 8459

John Q. Public
123 Money Lane
Richmondville, NC 27710
123-456-7890
8458

Date _____, 20_____

Pay to
the order of _____ | $ [＿＿＿＿]

_____ Dollars

Bank of America.

Sample only. Not negotiable.

MEMO _____

A011000010A 09876543210C 8460

John Q. Public
123 Money Lane
Richmondville, NC 27710
123-456-7890
8459

Date _____, 20_____

Pay to
the order of _____ | $ [＿＿＿＿]

_____ Dollars

Bank of America.

Sample only. Not negotiable.

MEMO _____

A011000010A 09876543210C 8461

READING 16.1 About Checking Accounts

A checking account provides certain **benefits**:

▲ It is safer than carrying or mailing cash.

▲ It makes day-to-day money transactions easier to handle.

▲ It can be less expensive than using money orders or check-cashing services.

▲ It provides a good record of purchases or expenditures. Paid checks serve as proof of payment. Monthly statements track where money was spent.

▲ It helps people establish a good financial record with a financial institution.

Checking accounts come with certain **features and costs**. Be sure to ask the following questions:

▲ Does the account pay interest? If so, what balance is required to earn interest?

▲ Are there monthly service charges and/or per-check charges?

▲ What are the fees for such items as: printed checks, use of the ATM, overdrafts (check written without sufficient funds in account), stop payment (request by a depositor for the bank not to pay a check that he or she has written)?

▲ Is there a "free checking" account? What are the requirements for such an account?

If you open a checking account, you take on certain responsibilities. It is your responsibility to:

▲ Protect your checkbook and ATM card to guard against theft.

▲ Write checks correctly to prevent tampering or forgery.

▲ Keep a running total and balance your account monthly to avoid overdrafts.

READING 16.2

Opening a Checking Account

1 **Choose a financial institution offering a checking account that fits your needs.**
Financial institutions vary in the types of checking accounts that they offer. Choose a financial institution that offers a checking account that you believe is best for you and is convenient for you to use.

2 **Take identification to the bank officer handling new accounts.** Make sure to take a copy of your driver's license, an official state identification card, or a birth certificate, as well as your Social Security number. If it is to be a joint account, bring information for the second person as well. A joint account will give the other individual equal access to the money in the account. Financial institutions usually require a parent or other adult to be named on the account (joint account) if you are under 18 years.

3 **Provide the bank officer with information, including:**
▲ Current address and phone number. This is so the bank knows where to send your monthly statement and how to reach you if there are questions.
▲ Social Security number, mother's maiden name, and your birthplace. This provides the bank with information that only you know, so that you are protected in case someone tries to use, or seek information about, your account.

4 **Complete a signature card.**
The bank will keep this card as a sample of your signature(s) to protect against unauthorized individuals using your account. If you select an interest-bearing account, you will be asked to sign a W-9 Form, which will allow the bank to pay interest without withholding tax.

5 **Make an opening deposit.** You will need to deposit at least the minimum amount required by that financial institution.

6 **Read and review the disclosures that the bank officer will give you.**
These are important materials that cover such areas as how interest is paid on an interest-bearing account, how to order checks, how to set up and use an ATM card, and other rules about the account.

Ten Tips for ATM Safety

1   **Stay alert.** Be aware of your surroundings when you use an ATM, especially at night. It's best to only use an ATM in a well-lighted area and have someone accompany you.

2   **Report suspicious activity.** If you notice anything unusual, cancel your transaction, pocket your card, and leave immediately. Go to a safe place and call the police if you suspect dangerous or illegal activity.

3   **Be prepared.** To complete your transaction safely, fill out your account deposit forms and have your card ready before arriving at the ATM. When you've completed your transaction, pocket your card, receipt, and cash immediately. It is unwise to openly count cash in front of others.

4   **Take special precautions at drive-up ATMs.** When using a drive-up ATM, remember always to keep your doors locked, all other windows rolled up, and the car running.

5   **Treat your ATM card like cash.** Guard your ATM card as carefully as you do cash, checks, and credit cards. Never give account numbers, card information, or your PIN over the phone.

6   **Keep your personal identification number (PIN) secret.** Don't write your PIN on your card or keep it in your wallet. Memorize your number and do not tell anyone what it is—even family members and bank employees.

7   **Be courteous while waiting at an ATM.** Keep a polite distance from the person using the ATM before you. Allow that person to complete the transaction before you approach the machine.

8   **Protect your privacy.** Be mindful of others waiting behind you. Position yourself in front of the ATM keyboard to prevent someone from observing your PIN.

9   **Save your ATM receipts.** Remember to record each transaction in your checkbook register and match it to your monthly statement. Do not leave receipts at the ATM; they may contain confidential information.

10   **Report a lost or stolen card immediately.** Call the bank as soon as you realize your card has been lost or stolen, so the bank can cancel your lost card and begin the process of issuing you a new card. The telephone number to call is usually listed on your statement.

170

ASSESSMENT
16.1

What's Great About Our Checking Accounts?

As the new public relations manager for a local bank, you've been asked to develop an advertisement stating the virtues of your bank and the checking accounts it offers. Contact a local bank, savings and loan, or credit union by phone or online to gather information on the available checking accounts. Be sure to include strengths of the financial institution, such as location and banking hours, and the specific features of the accounts. Use the following list of features and costs to develop your advertisement.

Checking Account Features and Costs:

▲ Monthly fees

▲ Minimum balance needed to avoid paying a monthly fee

▲ Per-check charges

▲ Penalty fees for overdrafts

▲ ATM charges

▲ Stop-payment fees

▲ Charges for printed checks

▲ Availability of overdraft protection

▲ Interest rates on interest-bearing accounts

LESSON 17
What Taxes Affect You?

Warm-Up

Everybody likes to drive on smooth roads and enjoy the beauty of national parks. Everybody wants good schools, safe neighborhoods, and clean streets. Everybody would like to enjoy these benefits, but who pays for them?

You have already learned that every benefit has a cost. The cost for highway construction and forest maintenance or for police and fire protection is great. Where does the money come from to pay for the resources necessary to maintain beauty and safety in your city, your state, or the whole U.S.A.?

If you answered *taxes,* you're correct. Different kinds of taxes are used to fund the projects that citizens want. For example:

▲ Property (real estate) taxes help pay for local schools.

▲ Federal income taxes are used to fund our national defense program.

▲ State income taxes go toward parks and social services.

▲ Local sales taxes pay for the upkeep of libraries.

▲ Toll-road fees are a tax too; they are used to maintain highways.

MUSCLE DEVELOPERS
Learn these ideas, practice them, and develop your financial fitness muscles.

✔ Taxes are used to provide services that benefit all citizens.

✔ There are several kinds of taxes: income, sales, property.

✔ Most consumers in the United States pay taxes on goods and services they buy— telephone service, gas for the car, clothing, toys and a fast-food meal.

✔ Most workers in the United State have to pay income taxes.

✔ Income taxes, social security taxes, retirement account contributions, and other deductions are subtracted regularly from a worker's paycheck.

✔ Every year, by April 15th, most people must complete a federal income tax form that lists their income and the amount of tax that they owe.

✔ Income taxes are calculated as a percent of a worker's income; people who earn more income usually pay a higher percentage than those who earn less income.

FITNESS VOCABULARY

Gross pay – Total wages for total hours worked.

Net pay – Amount of wages received after all deductions have been taken into account.

Take-home pay – Same as net pay.

Payroll deduction – Amount of money automatically subtracted from gross pay for taxes, insurance, retirement benefits, etc.

IRS – Internal Revenue Service; the agency that collects federal income taxes.

Income tax – A tax on earnings; every worker who earns a certain amount must pay federal income taxes. (Some states and cities also have their own income taxes.)

Real estate property tax – A tax paid by people who own homes, business properties, condominiums, or other real estate. Property tax may also be charged on personal property, such as boats or cars.

Transfer payments – Payments by government to people who do not currently perform productive services.

FICA – Federal Insurance Contributions Act (more commonly called *social security*). This is a transfer tax because it transfers money from people who are working to those who no longer work.

Showing Your Strength

If you know the answers to these questions, you are developing some financial muscle.

1 **Does everyone have to pay income tax?** *(No. A person who earns below a certain amount pays no income tax. Also, persons who have many deductions and exemptions may pay little or no income tax.)*

2 **How are income taxes calculated?** *(The IRS [Internal Revenue Service] has rules for how much income tax a person owes. This amount is based on the amount of money you earn in one year. The higher your income, the higher the percentage of income tax you will have to pay.)*

3 **Why are income taxes deducted from paychecks all year long?** *(The government needs money every day to provide services. By deducting taxes regularly, it collects operating income as the year progresses. Also, some people might not plan ahead and save the money they would need to pay their taxes on April 15th. Regular tax deductions act as a forced saving plan to pay taxes.)*

173

4 **Who receives social security benefits?** *(Retired persons are eligible for social security benefits if they have worked long enough. There are also benefits for people who are disabled and can't work, and for families in which a parent has died.)*

5 **Who pays social security taxes?** *(Nearly all workers pay social security taxes as well as the employers for whom they work.)*

6 **What is a sales tax?** *(A sales tax is a consumption tax. It is paid at the time a product is purchased. Usually the sales tax is a percentage of the price of a product. A sales tax is set by individual states and cities.)*

7 **What are transfer payments?** *(The government makes transfer payments to people who do not currently perform productive services. Social security, unemployment compensation, and public assistance are examples of transfer payments.)*

8 **What is a real estate property tax?** *(Property taxes are assessed, or levied, on homes, business properties, or other real estate by a state, county, or city. Property taxes are often used to support public schools, libraries, parks, and other public institutions. Real estate property tax is an important source of revenue for local governments.)*

Department of the Treasury — Internal Revenue Service

Form 1040 **U.S. Individual Income Tax Return**

For the year Jan 1-Dec 31, 2000, or other tax year beginn

Label (See instructions.)

Your First Name MI Last Nam

If a Joint Return, Spouse's First Name MI Last Nar

Use the IRS label. Otherwise, please print or type.

Home Address (number and street). If You Have a P.O. Box, See

City, Town or Post Office. If You Have a Foreign Address, See I

Presidential Election Campaign (See instructions.)

Note: Checking 'Yes' will not change your tax
Do you, or your spouse if filing a joint return,

Filing Status

Check only one box.

1 Single
2 Married filing joint return (even if only
3 Married filing separate return. Enter sp
4 Head of household (with qualifying pe
dependent, enter this child's name he
5 Qualifying widow(er) with dependent

Exemptions

6a Yourself. If your parent (or someone
her tax return, do not check box 6a

b Spouse ....

c Dependents:

(1) First name Last name

If more than six dependents, see instructions.

d Total number of exemptions claimed

Income

Attach Forms W-2 and W-2G here. Also attach Form(s) 1099-R if tax was withheld.

If you did not get a W-2, see instructions.

Enclose, but do not attach, any payment. Also, please use Form 1040-V.

7 Wages, salaries, tips, etc. Attach For
8a Taxable interest. Attach Schedule B
b Tax-exempt interest. Do not include
9 Ordinary dividends. Attach Schedule
10 Taxable refunds, credits, or offsets
11 Alimony received ....
12 Business income or (loss). Attach Sched
13 Capital gain or (loss). Attach Sched
14 Other gains or (losses). Attach For
15a Total IRA distributions 15a
16a Total pensions & annuities . 16a
17 Rental real estate, royalties, partn
18 Farm income or (loss). Attach Sch
19 Unemployment compensation ...
20a Social security benefits 20
21 Other income. List type & amount (see in
22 Add the amounts in the far right

Adjusted Gross Income

23 IRA deduction (see instructions)
24 Student loan interest deduction
25 Medical savings account deduct
26 Moving expenses. Attach Form
27 One-half of self-employment ta
28 Self-employed health insurance
29 Self-employed SEP, SIMPLE,
30 Penalty on early withdrawal of
31a Alimony paid b Recipient's SSN ....
32 Add lines 23 through 31a .....
33 Subtract line 32 from line 22.

BAA For Disclosure, Privacy Act, and Paperwork Red

Financial Fitness for Life: Shaping Up Your Financial Future Student Workouts, ©National Council on Economic Education

READING 17.1

Is This a Road or a Parking Lot?

Tony's family owned a hardware store in town. The store was established nearly 75 years ago by Tony's great-grandparents. As a child, Tony would visit his great-grandparents who lived in an apartment above the store. For his great-grandparents, it was a convenient place to live; they could simply walk down the stairs to get to work each morning.

Tony's grandparents worked in the hardware store too. They lived in a house several blocks away from the store. They would drive about five minutes through side streets to arrive at work. This was not the case for Tony's mom. Tony's dad wanted to live in a more country-like setting, so his parents bought a small farm far outside the town. They bought their farmhouse quite a few years before Tony was born. He couldn't imagine living anywhere else. For years, Tony's mom drove to and from the hardware store with very little trouble. It took about 20 minutes for the drive.

Five years ago, however, everything changed. Two large businesses were invited to town. These businesses promised to provide more than 3,000 jobs. They kept that promise, and then some. Now the town is bustling with thousands of cars on the roads, and new houses are going up everywhere, even all around Tony's family's farm. Everyone in the town, including Tony's family, agrees that the new businesses are the best thing that ever happened in the town. The stores are flourishing. There are plenty of kids to fill ball teams and the local youth clubs, and Tony's class is bursting with more than 80 students. Tony can't even count all of his friends.

However, there is a downside. Tony's mom drives on the same roads she has for 20 years, but the drive that once took only 20 minutes now takes, at least, 40 minutes. The townspeople are desperate for a new highway to go around the town. No private company would be willing to build a highway because it wouldn't be profitable. How could they charge each driver entering the road? They would have to set up tollbooths and allow very limited access to the road. In Tony's community, this just wouldn't be practical. Tony's mom and the rest of the drivers could go door to door asking residents to contribute voluntarily to a new road. They figure that plan wouldn't work, either. Some people wouldn't consider the road important, so they wouldn't contribute. That would leave the cost to be funded to those who wanted the road.

Would private funding of the road be fair, considering that many people would use the road even if they did not contribute?

_____

_____

_____

_____

How will the townspeople get this badly needed road?

_____

_____

_____

How does your community get new roads constructed?

_____

_____

_____

Where Did the Money Go?

Study the paycheck stub to answer the questions that follow:

Employee name:	John Taxpayer
Employee Social Security Number:	123-45-6789
Pay period Ending:	12-31-02

Total wages:	$2,823.08
Federal Tax Withheld (based on exemptions claimed on Form W-4):	541.73
State Taxes:	115.00
Local Taxes:	25.00
Social Security Tax and Medicare Tax Withheld (FICA):	210.00
Total deductions from paycheck:	$892.34
Net Pay (the amount of your paycheck):	$1,930.74

1 What do you report on a Form W-4?

2 For what purposes are state taxes collected?

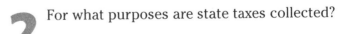

3 For what purposes are federal taxes collected?

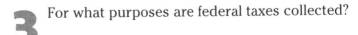

4 Are FICA and federal income tax used to pay for the same things? Explain. _____

_____

_____

177

NOTES

NOTES

NOTES

NOTES

181

NOTES